OFFICIAL PREPARATION MATERIAL

Cambridge English

Objective First

Teacher's Book
with Teacher's Resources CD-ROM

Annette Capel   Wendy Sharp

Fourth Edition

CAMBRIDGE
UNIVERSITY PRESS

University Printing House, Cambridge CB2 8BS, United Kingdom

Cambridge University Press is part of the University of Cambridge.

It furthers the University's mission by disseminating knowledge in the pursuit of education, learning and research at the highest international levels of excellence.

www.cambridge.org
Information on this title: www.cambridge.org/9781107628359

First edition © Cambridge University Press 2000
Second edition © Cambridge University Press 2008
Third edition © Cambridge University Press 2012
Fourth edition © Cambridge University Press and UCLES 2014

First published 2000
Second edition 2008
Third edition 2012
Fourth edition 2014
Reprinted 2014

Printed in Poland by Opolgraf

A catalogue for this publication is available from the British Library

ISBN 978-1-107-62835-9   Teacher's Book with Teacher's Resources CD-ROM
ISBN 978-1-107-62834-2   Student's Book without answers with CD-ROM
ISBN 978-1-107-62830-4   Student's Book with answers with CD-ROM
ISBN 978-1-107-62854-0   Class Audio CDs (2)
ISBN 978-1-107-62839-7   Workbook without answers with Audio CD
ISBN 978-1-107-62845-8   Workbook with answers with Audio CD
ISBN 978-1-107-62856-4   Student's Pack (Student's Book without answers with CD-ROM, Workbook without answers with Audio CD)
ISBN 978-1-107-62847-2   Student's Book Pack (Student's Book with answers with CD-ROM and Class Audio CDs (2))
ISBN 978-1-107-29696-1   Student's Book ebook
ISBN 978-1-107-62857-1   Presentation Plus DVD-ROM

Additional resources for this publication at www.cambridge.org/elt/objectivefirstnew

Cover concept by Tim Elcock

Produced by Hart McLeod

Contents

Teacher's Resources CD-ROM

12 Progress tests

Wordlist with definitions

Wordlist without definitions

B1 Phrasal verbs students should know

Map of Objective First Student's Book

TOPIC	EXAM PRACTICE	GRAMMAR	VOCABULARY
Unit 1 **Fashion matters** 10–13 Fashion; describing people	Paper 4 Speaking: 2 Paper 3 Listening: 3 Paper 1 Reading and Use of English: 4	Comparison: adjectives and adverbs Adverbs of degree	APPEARANCE AND CLOTHING Phrasal verbs
Exam folder 1 14–15	Paper 1 Reading and Use of English: 4 Key word transformations		
Unit 2 **The virtual world** 16–19 Computer games; the internet	Paper 1 Reading and Use of English: 7	*-ly* adverbs Review of present tenses	COMPUTERS Collocations Word formation
Writing folder 1 20–21	Paper 2 Writing: 2 Informal letters		
Unit 3 **Going places** 22–25 Travel	Paper 4 Speaking: 2 Paper 3 Listening: 2 Paper 1 Reading and Use of English: 1 and 4	Modals 1: Obligation, necessity and permission Prepositions of location	TRAVEL AND HOLIDAYS Topic set – travel and holidays Phrasal verbs Collocations
Exam folder 2 26–27	Paper 1 Reading and Use of English: 3 Word formation		
Unit 4 **Endangered** 28–31 Animals	Paper 1 Reading and Use of English: 7 Paper 1 Reading and Use of English: 4	*as* and *like* Compound adjectives	ANIMALS Word formation Topic set – parts of animals Expressions with *time*
Writing folder 2 32–33	Paper 2 Writing: 1 Essays		
Unit 5 **Mixed emotions** 34–37 Describing frightening and positive experiences	Paper 3 Listening: Skills for Listening Paper 1 Reading and Use of English: 2	Review of past tenses: past simple past continuous present perfect past perfect Irregular verbs	EMOTIONS Collocations – adverbs of degree
Exam folder 3 38–39	Paper 1 Reading and Use of English: 2 Open cloze		
Unit 6 **What if?** 40–43 Winning prizes and celebrity culture	Paper 1 Reading and Use of English: 6 Paper 1 Reading and Use of English: 1 and 3 Paper 4 Speaking: 4	Conditionals with *if* Conditionals with *unless* Parts of speech	WINNING AND CELEBRITY Phrasal verbs with *keep* Word formation
Writing folder 3 44–45	Paper 2 Writing: 2 Reports		
Units 1–6 Revision 46–47			
Unit 7 **Life's too short** 48–51 Sport	Paper 1 Reading and Use of English: 3 and 4 Paper 3 Listening: 3 Paper 4 Speaking: 3	Gerunds and infinitives 1	SPORT Collocations – sports Expressions with *do* Word formation
Exam folder 4 52–53	Paper 1 Reading and Use of English: 1 Multiple-choice cloze		
Unit 8 **Growing up** 54–57 Childhood	Paper 4 Speaking: 2 and 4 Paper 1 Reading and Use of English: 5 Paper 1 Reading and Use of English: 3	*used to* and *would*	JOBS AND WORK Collocations Phrasal verbs with *get* Word formation
Writing folder 4 58–59	Paper 2 Writing: 1 Essays		

TOPIC	EXAM PRACTICE	GRAMMAR	VOCABULARY
Unit 18 **What's in a book?** 116–119 Books	Paper 1 Reading and Use of English: 5 Paper 3 Listening: 3 Paper 1 Reading and Use of English: 2 and 4	*enough, too, very, so, such*	BOOKS Phrasal verbs with *come* and *go*
Writing folder 9 120–121	Paper 2 Writing: 2 Reviews		
Units 13–18 Revision 122–123			
Unit 19 **An apple a day …** 124–127 Health and fitness	Paper 4 Speaking: 2 and 4 Paper 3 Listening: 4 Paper 1 Reading and Use of English: 1	Modals 3: Advice and suggestion *It's time* *have/get something done*	THE BODY AND HEALTH Topic set – parts of the body Phrases with *on* Word formation Topic set – health
Exam folder 10 128–129	Paper 1 Reading and Use of English: 5 Multiple choice – fiction		
Unit 20 **No place to hide** 130–133 Crime	Paper 1 Reading and Use of English: 6	Gerunds and infinitives 2	CRIME Topic set – crime
Writing folder 10 134–135	Paper 2 Writing: 2 Emails		
Unit 21 **Urban decay, suburban hell** 136–139 City life	Paper 4 Speaking: 2 and 4 Paper 3 Listening: 2 Paper 1 Reading and Use of English: 1	Mixed conditionals	CITY LIFE Collocations Topic set – buildings Word formation
Exam folder 11 140–141	Paper 1 Reading and Use of English: 7 Multiple matching		
Unit 22 **A world of music** 142–145 Music	Paper 4 Speaking: 2 Paper 1 Reading and Use of English: 6 Paper 1 Reading and Use of English: 1	Concessive clauses Complex sentences	MUSIC Topic set – music
Writing folder 11 146–147	Paper 2 Writing: 2 Reports		
Unit 23 **Unexpected events** 148–151 Natural disasters	Paper 3 Listening: 2 Paper 1 Reading and Use of English: 2 and 4	*I wish / If only* *wish / hope*	THE NATURAL WORLD Phrasal verbs with *off* Words often confused Word formation Topic set – weather
Exam folder 12 152–153	Paper 1 Reading and Use of English: 5 Multiple choice – non-fiction		
Unit 24 Anything for a laugh 154–157 Humour	Paper 4 Speaking: 2 Paper 1 Reading and Use of English: 7 Paper 1 Reading and Use of English: 2	*rather* The grammar of phrasal verbs	HUMOUR
Writing folder 12 158–159	Paper 2 Writing: 2 Articles		
Units 19–24 Revision 160–161			
Speaking folder 162–163			
Phrasal verb list 164–165			
Grammar folder 166–176			

Content of the Cambridge English: First

The *Cambridge English: First* examination consists of four papers. The Reading and Use of English paper carries 40% of the marks, while the Writing, Listening and Speaking papers each carry 20% of the marks. It is not necessary to pass all four papers in order to pass the examination. If you achieve a grade A in the examination, you will be awarded a *Cambridge English: First* certificate at C1 level. If you achieve grade B or C, you will be awarded a *Cambridge English: First* certificate at B2 level. If your performance is below B2, but falls within Level B1, you will get a *Cambridge English* certificate stating that you demonstrated ability at B1 level.

As well as being told your grade, you will also be given a Statement of Results – a graphical profile of your performance, i.e. it will show whether you have done especially well or badly on some of the papers.

Paper 1 Reading and Use of English 1 hour 15 minutes

There are seven parts to this paper and they are always in the same order. The first four parts test your grammar and vocabulary. The last three parts each contain a text and a comprehension task. The texts used are from newspaper and magazine articles, fiction and reviews.

Part	Task type	Number of questions	Task format	Objective Exam folder
1	Multiple choice gap-fill, mainly testing vocabulary	8	You must choose which word from four answers completes each of the eight gaps in a text.	**4** (52–53)
2	Open gap-fill, testing mainly grammar	8	You must complete a text with eight gaps.	**3** (38–39)
3	Word formation	8	You need to use the right form of a given word to fill the gaps in a text containing eight gaps.	**2** (26–27)
4	Key word transformations testing grammar and vocabulary	6	You must complete a sentence with a given word, so that it means the same as the first sentence.	**1** (14–15)
5	Multiple choice	6	You must read a text and answer multiple-choice questions with four options: A, B, C or D.	Fiction **10** (128–129) Non-fiction **12** (152–153)
6	Gapped text	6	You must read a text with sentences removed. You need to use the missing sentences to complete the text.	**9** (114–115)
7	Multiple matching	10	You must answer the questions by finding the relevant information in the text or texts.	**11** (140–141)

Paper 2 Writing 1 hour 20 minutes

There are two parts to this paper. Part 1 is compulsory, you have to answer it. In Part 2 there are three questions and you must choose one. Each part carries equal marks and you are expected to write between 140–190 words for Part 1 and 140–190 for Part 2.

Part	Task type	Number of tasks	Task format	Objective Writing folder
1	Question 1 Writing an essay	1 compulsory	An essay presented through rubric and short notes.	**2** (32–33); **4** (58–59); **8** (108–109)
2	Questions 2–4 • an article • a letter or email • a report • a review	One task to be selected from a choice of three	You are given a choice of topics and you have to respond to one of them in the way specified.	Informal letters and emails **1** (20–21); **10** (134–5) Letters of application **7** (96–97); Articles **5** (70–71); **12** (158–159); Reviews **6** (82–83); **9** (120–121); Reports **3** (44–45); **11** (146–147)

Paper 3 Listening about 40 minutes

There are four parts to this paper. Each part is heard twice. The texts are a variety of types with either one speaker or more than one.

Part	Task type	Number of questions	Task format	Objective Exam folder
1	Multiple choice	8	You hear short, unrelated extracts, each about 30 seconds, with either one or two speakers. You must choose an answer from A, B or C.	**6** (76–77)
2	Sentence completion	10	You hear one speaker and this part lasts about three minutes. You must write a word or short phrase to complete the sentences.	**5** (64–65)
3	Multiple matching	5	You hear five unrelated extracts with a common theme. Each lasts about 30 seconds. You must choose the correct answer from a list of eight.	**7** (90–91)
4	Multiple choice	7	You hear an interview or a conversation of about three minutes. You must choose an answer from A, B or C.	**8** (102–103)

Paper 4 Speaking about 14 minutes

There are four parts to this paper. There are usually two of you taking the examination and two examiners. This paper tests your accuracy, vocabulary, pronunciation and your ability to communicate and complete the tasks.

Part	Task type	Time	Format	Objective Speaking folder
1	The interviewer asks each candidate some questions.	2 minutes	You are asked to give information about yourself.	Speaking folder (162–163)
2	Each candidate talks to the interviewer for about 1 minute.	4 minutes	You have to talk about two pictures and then comment on the other candidate's pictures.	Speaking folder (162–163)
3	Candidates have to discuss a task together.	4 minutes	You are given some material in the form of a discussion question and five prompts, presented as a mind map, to discuss with the other candidate.	Speaking folder (162–163)
4	Candidates offer opinions relating to the task they have just completed.	4 minutes	The interviewer will join in with your discussion.	Speaking folder (162–163)

Introduction to the Fourth Edition

2015 examination

All of the material in the Student's Book and in the other components of the course has been fully updated to reflect the new specifications of the *Cambridge English: First*. The revised examination comprises four papers and is now slightly shorter at around 3.5 hours. For full information on these specifications, visit the Cambridge English Language Assessment website, http://www.cambridgeenglish.org, where you can download the official handbook.

Course components

Student's Book with CD-ROM

The Student's Book contains 24 topic-based units, to encourage a sense of pace and achievement. On the accompanying CD-ROM there are 96 exercises, eight for each pair of units, giving extra practice in grammar, vocabulary, listening, reading and writing. The CD-ROM also has unit wordlists with and without definitions.

Workbook with Audio CD

The Workbook offers further practice in grammar, vocabulary, reading and writing as well as 12 listening exam practice tasks on the audio component.

Teacher's Book with Teacher's Resources CD-ROM

The Teacher's Resources CD-ROM that accompanies the Teacher's Book includes a selection of photocopiable resources: 12 progress tests, wordlists with and without definitions, and a list of B1 phrasal verbs for review purposes, taken from the *English Vocabulary Profile*.

Webpage

The dedicated webpage is:
www.cambridge.org/elt/objectivefirstnew.
On this page you will find a number of useful resources for both students and teachers:

- Photocopiable *Cambridge English: First* Practice Tests with audio
- Photocopiable unit-by-unit wordlists

Presentation Plus

Presentation Plus interactive whiteboard software allows teachers to present and interact directly with the Student's Book, Workbook and Class Audio at the front of the classroom. With Presentation Plus you can highlight, write and erase; hide and reveal text and images; zoom in and out; create notes and save annotations; attach your own web links; display answer keys; play all Class Audio and display the listening scripts; and connect to Cambridge Dictionaries Online via the internet. Presentation Plus can be used with all types of interactive whiteboards or with a computer and projector.

English Profile

English Profile is a long-term research programme that is seeking to describe what learners know and can do in English at each level of the Common European Framework of Reference (CEFR). The CEFR is 'language-neutral', as it is designed to work for all languages. A number of *English Profile* projects, initially targeting grammar, functions and vocabulary, will illustrate in detail what the CEFR means for English. A key feature of *English Profile* is the extensive use it makes of various corpora of language data, including the largest analysed corpus of learner data in the world: the *Cambridge Learner Corpus*. This contains learner writing at all levels of the CEFR from over 200 countries.

English Vocabulary Profile

Over five years in research and development, the *English Vocabulary Profile* is an interactive web resource that provides detailed information on the words, phrases, phrasal verbs and idioms that are known by learners at each level of the CEFR. There are around 4700 headword entries up to B2 level (7000 to C2 level) and each entry presents individual meanings of a word in CEFR order, to suggest learning priorities. For example, the entry for the word *stage* has the meaning THEATRE – the raised area in a theatre where actors perform – at A2 and PART – a period of development, or a particular time in a process – at B2.

The *English Vocabulary Profile* lists many phrases within its entries, so the entry for the noun *way* includes *by the way* at A2 and useful phrases such as *one way or another*, *make your way* and *in a way* at B2. Phrasal verbs are included at the end of an entry, and it is possible to search for words, phrases, phrasal verbs and idioms as separate categories by level – interestingly, only twelve idioms are included at B2, with many more featuring at C1 and C2.

How has *Objective First* been informed by the *English Vocabulary Profile*?

Having access to the online resource during the writing of the last edition enabled us to check the level of all the vocabulary used in the course, as well as providing us with additional level-appropriate words and phrases for individual units.

The Vocabulary sections in *Objective First* focus on the areas of development that are important for learners working towards B2 and, in particular, for students preparing for the *Cambridge English: First* examination. There are regular sections on phrases and collocations, word formation, phrasal verbs and topic vocabulary, all informed by the *English Vocabulary Profile*. Find out more by visiting www.englishprofile.org.

1 Fashion matters

1.1

Exam skills	Speaking Paper 4 Part 2
	Listening Paper 3 Part 3
Vocabulary	Appearance, clothing and the
	fashion industry
	Phrasal verbs

1.2

Grammar focus	Comparison
Grammar extra	Adverbs of degree
Exam skills	Reading and Use of English Paper 1
	Part 4

Workbook contents

Spelling
Phrasal verbs
Reading – comprehension, superlatives, vocabulary
Grammar – comparatives
Reading and Use of English Paper 1 Part 4 – key word
transformations

1.1 SB pages 10–11

Lesson plan

Throughout the Teacher's notes, approximate timings
are given for guidance. These relate to two lengths of
lesson: **SV** (short version), corresponding to a lesson of
60–70 minutes, and **LV** (long version), for a lesson of
around 90 minutes. Below these timings, there is always
an indication of what to cut out of the lesson (and set
for homework) for the short version or, conversely, what
to develop in the long version. Relevant suggestions for
extra activities are included in the notes.

Speaking	30–40 minutes
Listening	15–20 minutes
Vocabulary	20–30 minutes

SV	Spend less time on topic vocabulary in 2; set 8 for homework.
LV	See Extension activity for 1.

Speaking

1   The beginning of this lesson is conducted as pairwork.
Explain to students that for the Speaking test they
will be in pairs, with two examiners present. Refer
students to pages 6 and 7 of the Student's Book for
further information about this and other parts of the
examination.

Allow students around five minutes for this initial
discussion, which is an opportunity to warm up the
topic and talk about something familiar. If this is a new
class, the activity will also give you a chance to walk
round and make a quick assessment of their level and
speaking ability. It is normal at this stage of a course
for students to be nervous about speaking, so do
encourage them. Explain that by the end of the course,
their confidence will be sky-high!

Write up some useful sentence starters on the board:

Likes

I really like …
I prefer to wear …
What I absolutely love is …

Dislikes

I hate …
I wouldn't be seen dead in …

Extension activity

As an additional ice-breaker, bring in various items of clothing,
both men's and women's; if possible, try to get hold of some
obviously less fashionable items. Hold the clothes up one by one,
asking what they are and eliciting student preferences.

2   Ask students to describe people in other parts of the
classroom. This can be done as a guessing game, where
one student in the pair describes what a certain person
is wearing and the other says who is being described.
For a weaker class, start the activity off by describing
someone briefly in a couple of sentences and asking the
students who you are describing.

Students can then work in pairs or groups
brainstorming topic vocabulary. Ask them to make their
lists using the headings given. Allow enough time for
this (at least five minutes), as some of the vocabulary
will be needed for the subsequent Speaking and
Listening tasks. Some of the following vocabulary will
be useful:

Clothes: jeans, jacket, T-shirt, polo shirt
Footwear: trainers
Jewellery: necklace, ring
Headgear: hat, baseball cap
Materials: cotton, silk, polyester, suede, fur
Appearance: untidy, scruffy, fashionable

Discuss with students how to record new words in a vocabulary notebook. Topic vocabulary is often best learned in sets, with suitable headings like those above.

Teaching extra

Every unit in the course contains core topic vocabulary. Suggest students make posters for the classroom wall to help them remember some of this vocabulary. Store the posters after a unit is finished, and display them again at a later stage in the course (see Revision Unit notes on page 38). For Unit 1, a poster could be prepared for each of the headings given in 2, with pictures from magazines added.

3   In pairs, students take it in turns to describe each of the people in the pair of photographs they have chosen. Allow them up to three minutes for this and remind them to use the vocabulary they have just listed. They should not compare a pair of photographs yet.

4   Students now make comparisons between the people in the pair of photographs they have chosen. Refer them to the examples given, but encourage them to use their own ideas too.

5   Elicit some of these ideas and summarise what has been discussed by writing up a few sentences about each pair of photographs. Try to use different comparison structures on the board. Explain that the next lesson (1.2) will have a grammar focus, where these structures will be looked at and practised.

Listening

6   **1 02** Tell students that they are going to hear five short recordings, as an introduction to the matching task in Paper 3 Part 3. These will contain a variety of accents, as in the real exam.

The first recording is used as an example and students look at photo 3b while they listen. Then suggest that they read the transcript and think about the words in bold, to make them aware of the need to listen carefully. Before repeating the recording, explain that the checking of answers is an essential activity at the second listening in the exam.

Recording script

Speaker 1: I'm not a suit man. Even for work, I can get away with casual stuff, though I still like my clothes to look smart. I love shopping – my favourite place is Paul Smith in Covent Garden. I bought a really nice woollen shirt there recently. Clothes are important to me, but they need to be comfortable as well as stylish.

1 03 Ask students to listen to the four remaining extracts and match the photos to the speakers. They should do this on their own and only compare answers when they have finished. Only play the recording a second time if they need to check their answers. (They will listen to the four extracts again in 7.)

Answers
Speaker 2 – 2a	Speaker 3 – 1a
Speaker 4 – 4b	Speaker 5 – 3a

Recording script

Speaker 2: I started working this year, so I'm able to get new clothes more regularly than before, when I had to save up for months. I buy a lot online. My mum thinks I should cut down the amount I spend on clothes, but my image is really important to me: if someone sees me in something once, I don't like to go out in it again – well, not for a while, in any case. I like to wear bright colours and my make-up's a bit outrageous. I always dress up when I go clubbing. I buy a big range of styles and I try to keep up with the latest fashions.

Speaker 3: Shopping for clothes isn't really my scene, if you know what I mean. I don't really mind what I wear, to tell you the truth. I'm the least fashion-conscious person I know! I suppose if anything I favour the casual look. I've got two pairs of jeans and I wear them mostly with a sweatshirt or something. I have got one favourite T-shirt, which a girlfriend gave me. It's red and it's got a sort of abstract design printed in navy blue on the back. She said she gave it to me so I would always stand out in a crowd!

Speaker 4: My clothes have to be comfortable, make me feel relaxed as soon as I slip them on. I often put together outfits from stuff I find in street markets – they're less expensive that way. Second-hand clothes can be real bargains, and usually they've hardly been worn! I'll change the look of my clothes quite frequently, you know, sew in a new piece of material, swap buttons, dye something a different colour, just for a change. I make a lot of my own jewellery, though having long hair, I don't wear earrings very often.

Speaker 5: My friends take far less trouble with clothes than I do – sometimes they wear the tattiest things ever! As my job involves dealing with people, I have to make an effort to look good all the time. I like to present a classy, sophisticated image. I go shopping for clothes about once a month, though if I see something by chance, I'm quite likely to go for it there and then. I think I've got good taste and I very rarely make a mistake when I buy clothes. I did take a jacket back last week, but that was because it was badly made.

Vocabulary

English profile

The fourth edition of *Objective First* has been informed by the *English Vocabulary Profile*, a detailed description of the words and phrases that are known by learners at each level of the Common European Framework of Reference (CEFR). *English Profile* is a collaborative programme to enhance the learning, teaching and assessment of English worldwide and its main funding partners are Cambridge University Press and Cambridge English Language Assessment. For more information, visit www.englishprofile.org

7 Start by checking how much students know about phrasal verbs. Explain that these are very common, particularly in informal, spoken English. Play the recording for Speakers 2–5 again and ask students to tick the phrasal verbs they hear. Elicit these and write them up on the board. Then ask students to match them to the short definitions. (The numbers in brackets refer to the Speakers.)

Answers

The phrasal verbs heard are: cut down   dress up
go out   keep up with   put together   save up
slip on   stand out   take back

a stand out (3)
b put together (4)
c take back (5)
d dress up (2)
e save up (2)
f cut down (2)
g slip on (4)
h go out (2)
i keep up with (2)

Corpus spot

The authors have referred extensively to the *Cambridge Learner Corpus*, an electronic collection of Cambridge English Language Assessment candidates' scripts from all over the world. Currently containing more than 45 million words of data, around 3 million words of recent candidate writing are added to the *Cambridge Learner Corpus* each year. This unique resource has given the authors a more accurate and up-to-date picture of what B2 learners around the world can and can't do.

8 Draw students' attention to the Corpus spot. Explain to students that phrasal verbs are often used more informally than one-word verbs with similar meaning.

Answers

a gone up
b going on
c went for
d went back
e go over
f go ahead

9

Answers

1 went out
2 slipped on
3 dressed up
4 put together
5 stood out
6 keep up with

10 Following the discussion, ask students to report their ideas to the class.

1.2 SB pages 12–13

Lesson plan	
Grammar focus	60–80 minutes
Grammar extra	10 minutes
SV	Set 8 for homework.
LV	Spend longer on discussion in 1; include the Extension activity after 5.

Comparison

1 Ask students to read the short text individually. Elicit students' views on the text. Is it still true that the fashion industry prefers to use the skinniest models? Why is this?

Point out that the text contains a number of superlative adjectives: *the youngest and skinniest, the most underweight, the least achievable.*

2 In this course, the approach to grammar is an inductive one. Students at this level have generally been taught all the basic structures and now need to review what they know. In most grammar focus lessons, students discuss examples and formulate explanations or rules. They can then check their understanding is correct by referring to the Grammar folder at the back of the Student's Book.

Ask students to look at the comparison structures given and discuss answers to the three questions in pairs. Allow them up to ten minutes for this, encouraging them to explore each question fully and make notes if appropriate. Refer students to the Grammar folder, page 166.

Answers

a Single-syllable adjectives add *-er/-est*; longer adjectives use *more / the most*.

b Some two-syllable adjectives, e.g. *common, likely, narrow, pleasant, simple, stupid*.

d Adjectives ending in a single vowel and consonant double the consonant (*slim → slimmer*); adjectives ending in *-y* change to *-ier/-iest*.

Corpus spot

Answers

a What are **the best** clothes to wear at the camp?
b He is **more famous** than all the others in the film.
c You look more tired and **thinner**.
d I would like to buy a **much better** one.
e It's now **easier** to get there.
f This is even **worse** than before.

---

3 Ask students to complete the table, working in pairs. Remind them to be careful about spelling.

Answers

bigger	the biggest
thinner	the thinnest
dirtier	the dirtiest
more/less casual	the most/least casual
more/less outrageous	the most/least outrageous
better	the best
worse	the worst

---

4 Allow students two or three minutes for this.

Answers

a brighter **b** the most outrageous / the brightest
c more casual **d** the dirtiest **e** thinner
f the worst **g** bigger **h** better

Grammar extra

In this course, these short sections cover additional small grammar points. They include some explanation and examples. There is usually a short exercise to practise the point, which can be set for homework if necessary.

Answers

a a bit; much
b a bit / a great deal / much; much (*much* can be used with both comparative and superlative adjectives)

---

5 Explain to students that the structure *not so ... as* is less common in everyday English nowadays. Allow them up to three minutes to compare the boots and shoes, using the words given.

Extension activity

In pairs, students can compare other 'designer' objects, such as mp3s/tablets or chairs (comfort/elegance).

---

6 Ask students to read the short article and identify the comparative adverbs. If they need help, remind them that most adverbs end in *-ly*. This will help students to locate them.

Answers

more commonly   more readily   less exclusively
less seriously

Refer students to the Grammar folder, page 166 or ask them to read this after class.

---

7 The discussion on counterfeit goods could be extended beyond fashion items to other goods, such as DVDs, computer games and perfume.

---

8 Explain that this exercise is an exam task from Paper 1 Part 4, key word transformations. This task type is introduced in detail in Exam folder 1, which follows Unit 1 (pages 14–15).

Make sure that students read the rubric carefully and remind them that they cannot use more than five words, including the word in bold.

Note that these transformations are below the level of the exam, as a first introduction to the task format.

Answers

1 were a bit cheaper / were a bit less expensive
2 the most talented designers
3 as straight as it
4 the least expensive of / less expensive than
5 more elegantly dressed than
6 is a lot quicker/faster than
7 less smartly when
8 as old as

Exam folder 1

SB pages 14–15

Paper 1 Part 4
Key word transformations

Remind students that there is a full description of the exam on pages 7–8 of the Student's Book. Paper 1 Reading and Use of English has seven parts and candidates have 1 hour and 15 minutes to complete the paper.

The Exam folders can be studied by students on their own outside class, but notes are given below for a mini-lesson in class.

1   Ask students to read the exam instructions carefully. They should then look at the example and the notes in italics.

Explain that there are two marks available, relating to the two parts of the answer. Therefore, even if students do not produce the whole answer, they can still get a mark if one element is accurate.

2   Ask students to close their books and to discuss in pairs what advice to give on this part of the exam. Allow them a couple of minutes to do this and suggest they make notes.

3   Now ask students to compare their notes with the advice given in the bullet points.

Stress that the key word must not be changed in any way. Check that students understand the information about contracted forms.

4   This task can either be set as homework or done in class.

Answers
1   told Sally about a new
2   took it back
3   make an effort
4   were not / weren't as fast as
5   much more easily if / when
6   far the most interesting

2 The virtual world

TOPIC Computer games; the internet

2.1

Exam skills	Reading – skimming and scanning
Vocabulary	Computers
	Collocations
	Word formation
Grammar extra	-ly adverbs

2.2

Grammar focus	Review of present tenses
Vocabulary	Word formation: prefixes and suffixes
	Positive and negative adjectives

Workbook contents

Listening Paper 3 Part 3 – multiple matching
Reading – skimming and scanning
Grammar – present tenses
Vocabulary – computer games; adjectives

2.1 SB pages 16–17

Lesson plan

Speaking	10–15 minutes
Reading	35–45 minutes
Grammar extra	10 minutes
Vocabulary	10–15 minutes

SV Shorten discussion in 1; set the Corpus spot for homework.

LV See Teaching extra.

Speaking

1 Exercises 1, 2 and 3 all provide opportunities for speaking, allowing you to find out what vocabulary students already know within the topic of computer games. Encourage them to talk about examples of different types of game, e.g. fantasy, combat, sport. Then refer students to the dictionary definition for *nerd* taken from the *Cambridge Learner's Dictionary*. Check understanding of this word and elicit students' reactions to the statement.

2 Ask students to discuss the question in groups. Then summarise on the board the advantages and disadvantages of playing online computer games.

3 Get students to spend up to five minutes deciding on the five most important features from a–h. This is a useful pre-reading task as a–h highlight some of the phrases from the texts. Elicit students' ideas of other important features.

Reading

Teaching extra

If your class has no previous experience of skimming and scanning skills, you may want to do some preliminary work with them before starting the Reading section. Make copies of the contents pages of three different magazines, for example one on cooking, one on computers, one on fashion. (The magazines don't have to be in English.) Divide the class into two groups, A and B. Explain that students in group A will attempt to read each contents page quickly to get a general idea of what all three magazines cover, while group B will have to search for articles on one specific topic, which is only dealt with in part of one magazine. Set a time limit of two minutes for this when you hand out the pages. At the end, ask group B to tell you which articles they have found. Then ask them what the other two magazines cover. If they have scanned as instructed, they will not be able to do this, because they will have focused on one section of the text only.

4 Explain that the skills of skimming and scanning are essential for Paper 1 Part 7 as time is limited. Ask students to scan the four reviews to find the answers to a–d. Elicit where the information is located.

Answers

a 4 Prices come at the end of 'The Verdict', at the foot of each review.
b 3 Five stars in The Verdict indicates this is the best review.
c 4 The Verdict says 'suitable for a very young audience'.
d 1 At the end of the review, it says the background music is 'truly original and builds well in scary moments'.

5 The purpose of this exercise is firstly to get students to skim quickly for general meaning. To encourage them, you could get the groups to compete to see which group is the first to be able to say briefly what sort of game each one is.

The second aim of the exercise is to show students how opinions are signposted in reviews. Explain to students that if they scan for key words and phrases, such as *the great thing about* and *it's a shame that*, they will find answers in texts more efficiently.

Before they begin, elicit the meaning of 'ray gun' in review 2. In science fiction stories a ray gun is an imaginary gun that fires energy in the form of heat or light rather than bullets. In this computer game it appears to be a device that can generate electricity and move and operate electrical appliances.

THE VIRTUAL WORLD 15

When students have found the good and bad points, get feedback from the groups and check they have identified the signposting language. (Review 4 contains the most.) Review some of this useful language on the board. Then have a class vote on which game seems the most appealing.

> **Answers**
>
> | **Good points** | **Bad points** |
> |---|---|
> | 1 | *you need to adopts its unique way of thinking* | *the absence of instructions (can also be a drawback)* |
> | | *the absence of instructions (part of the game's charm)* | |
> | | *original background music* | |
> | 2 | ***impressive** gameplay touches* | *It's a **shame** that the gun resets to weak* |
> | 3 | ***guarantees** a game demanding enough* | *motorbike games never provide the same thrill* |
> | | ***super-slick** bike racer* | |
> | 4 | ***nice** double-jump facility* | ***only** six levels* |
> | | ***really nice** background animation* | *a bit **disappointing*** |
> | | *Graphically, the game looks **good*** | *a slow rate* |
> | | | ***extremely boring*** |
> | | | *It's just **too bad** there isn't more content* |
> | | | *puzzles … far **too simple*** |

Vocabulary

6   Elicit the nouns that collocate with each verb. If time permits, ask students to brainstorm further nouns that collocate with *reach* and *take*. Suggest that students might list collocations like these in their vocabulary notebooks, adding to them over time.

> **Answers**
> a solve puzzles + a crime, a problem
> b spend (your) time + a fortune, money
> c reach the point (of) + a conclusion, a goal
> d take control + advantage (of), an interest (in)
>
> **Additional collocations:**
> reach + an agreement, a decision, a target
> take + account (of), charge, effect, part, place, pleasure (in), pride (in)

> ### **G**rammar extra
>
> Students can discuss this in pairs, referring to the Grammar folder, page 166 if they need help.
>
> > **Answers**
> > easy: remove -y; add -ily
> > endless: (regular) add -ly
> > graphic: add -ally NB This applies to all adjectives ending in -ic apart from *public*, which becomes *publicly*.
> > remarkable: remove e; add -y
> > true: remove e; add -ly

> a She hardly thought about work while she was on holiday. – *She didn't think about work much.*
> b He thought hard before answering. – *He thought carefully, for a long time.*
> c There have been a lot of good films lately. – *There have been a lot of good films recently.*
> d We arrived late for the film, which had already started. – *We arrived after the film had started.*

> ### **C**orpus spot
>
> > **Answers**
> > a **Unfortunately**, I'm quite busy at the moment.
> > b If I were you, I would **definitely** spend my evenings reading by the fireside.
> > c You just have to say your name and the computer opens the door **automatically**.
> > d Entering the restaurant, you **immediately** feel comfortable.
> > e We **really** started to work hard the morning before the show.
> > f You must adjust the laser **extremely** carefully to get it in the correct position.
> > g I would like more information, **especially** about accommodation.
> > h The computer **completely** takes hold of our lives.

2.2 SB pages 18–19

> **Lesson plan**
>
> | Grammar | 50–60 minutes |
> |---|---|
> | Vocabulary | 20–30 minutes |
>
> | SV | Set 5 and 8 for homework. |
> |---|---|
> | LV | See Extension activity in 7. |

Review of present tenses

1   Allow students 5–10 minutes to discuss the examples and complete the grammar explanation.

> **Answers**
> a present simple   c present simple
> b present continuous   d present continuous
>
> The present **simple** tense is used for permanent situations (example **a**) or to talk about actions which are habitual or repeated (example **c**). On the other hand, the present **continuous** tense is used for temporary situations (example **b**), or for situations that are changing or developing (example **d**).

2 Ask students to discuss the other uses shown in sentences a–e in pairs. Elicit their answers and then refer them to the Grammar folder on page 167.

Answers
a used for talking about an event in the near future (present continuous)
b used in the zero conditional (present simple)
c used for talking about something that is happening now (present continuous)
d used in a time clause (present simple)
e used for talking about something that is true (present simple)

3 Ask students to read sentences a–g carefully and correct any errors. Explain that some sentences are correct. They should give reasons why the corrections need to be made.

Answers
a ✓
b is selling (present continuous for a temporary situation)
c ✓
d play (present simple in a time clause)
e is giving (present continuous for a temporary situation)
f get (zero conditional)
g bookmark (present simple for a habitual or repeated action)

4 Ask students to work through the sentences on their own and then compare their answers in pairs.

Answers
a finish; get   **b** is improving   **c** are dealing with
d flies; explodes; hit   **e** is developing   **f** take
g log on; requires; generates
h crashes; lose; are working; save

5 Before reading the article, ask students to say how they use Google or another search engine.

Ask students to skim the article for general meaning and then do the gap-filling exercise on their own. Remind them to use a suitable present tense in each gap. When they have finished, they should compare answers and discuss the questions.

Answers
1	is becoming	7	sounds
2	are creating / create	8	believes
3	(are) updating / update	9	is encouraging
4	means	10	is changing
5	submits	11	find out
6	is adding / adds	12	google

The extra verb is *spend*.

Refer students to the list of stative verbs in the Grammar folder, page 167.

Vocabulary

6 Elicit the adjectives and spelling rules. If time permits, ask students to generate more adjectives ending in *-y* from nouns. Some examples are given below.

Answers
a tricky
b messy
c muddy (Rule: consonants *d, g, m, n, p, r, s, t* are doubled before adding *-y*)
d icy (Rule: *e* is removed before adding *-y*)
Additional nouns and adjectives:
blood – bloody	fun – funny	sun – sunny
curl – curly	juice – juicy	wind – windy
dust – dusty	noise – noisy	
fog – foggy	risk – risky	

7 Ask students to work in pairs to sort the adjectives, using a dictionary if necessary.

Answers
Positive: accessible, colourful, excellent, favourable, impressive, sophisticated
Negative: dull, hopeless, mindless, tricky, unhelpful
Unhelpful has both a prefix and a suffix.

ⓔxtension activity

English Profile research shows that students may only have met the prefix *un-* at B1 level; they are likely to know a few more suffixes at B1, including *-able, -ed, -ing, -y*. Give students the following words and ask them to identify their part of speech and then use *un-* and one of the four suffixes to form negative adjectives. Students can also write an example sentence for each adjective or, for greater challenge, a paragraph containing all five words.

believe   forget   health   interest   luck

Answers
believe (verb) unbelievable
forget (verb) unforgettable
health (noun) unhealthy
interest (noun or verb) uninterested/uninteresting
luck (noun) unlucky

8 Explain that there is a Word formation task on Paper 1 Reading and Use of English. This is a shorter version than the actual exam task, which has 8 questions. Advise students to look at the words around each gap to determine the part of speech that is required, and whether a singular or plural noun is needed (see question 2).

Answers
1	accessible (adjective)	4	impressive (adjective)
2	applications (noun)	5	electronically (adverb)
3	ability (noun)	6	tricky (adjective)

Writing folder 1

SB pages 20–21

Paper 2 Part 2 Informal letters

In Paper 2 Writing, it is important to write in a register that is suitable for the task set. Part 1 is a compulsory essay task requiring an unmarked or semi-formal register. In Part 2, where there is a choice of questions, there may be a letter or email task. If this is a letter of application, the register should be formal. If the task is a letter or email to a friend, it should be informal. Candidates at this level have problems in writing consistently in the appropriate register and Writing folder 1 addresses this issue.

1   Ask students to decide in pairs which two of the extracts are informal. Elicit informal words and phrases from these extracts and write them on the board.

> **Answers**
> **B** – get-together, It's a pity …, terrific, Why not …?
> **C** – Anyway …, Well …, weird guy, you'd better not, Why not …?, at my place

Refer students to the Assessment focus. Stress the importance in the exam of identifying the reader and the purpose of the letter or email. Then ask students to discuss possible writers, readers and purposes for extracts A–C.

> **Answers**
> **A** – department head to staff; report on the last meeting and a reminder about the next one
> **B** – departmental secretary to staff in department; invitation to next get-together
> **C** – friend to friend; invitation to stay for a party

2

> **Answers**
> Hi!, Guess what?, splash out, cool, I can't (contraction), a bit more.

3   Explain that when Paper 2 answers are marked, candidates are assessed in four areas: content, communicative achievement, organisation and language. The mark awarded for *content* will depend on how fully the target reader is informed in relation to the points given in the question. *Communicative achievement* covers the appropriacy of the register and format to the type of task set, and the effect of the piece of writing on the target reader. *Organisation* covers

how well organised the text is and the variety of linking words and cohesive devices used. *Language* focuses on both the range and accuracy of the vocabulary and structures used.

> **Answers**
> • failure to answer the question set (the answer ends up talking about something different)
> • inconsistent register (paragraphs 1 and 3)
> • poor organisation: long middle paragraph with an absence of linkers
> • language errors in middle paragraph

Ask students to quickly correct the errors in paragraph 2: you can't decide *whether* to buy; not as cheap *as*; choose *a* computer game; spend the money *on* something else.

The improvements to style in paragraphs 1 and 3 can be discussed quickly and written up after class if time is short.

4   Suggest that students plan their own letters in pairs, working through the ideas given under the C-L-O-S-E headings. Refer them also to the lists of phrases on page 21, which relate to this planning phase. Students often complain that they don't know what to write about. They need to think around the subject and plan what to say. This does not mean writing the whole piece in rough first. Stress that students don't have time to do this in the examination and it is not advisable – hurrying over a fair copy leads to words and even sentences being missed out, and leaves no time to check for errors.

Ask students to write the letter for homework, reminding them to write between 140 and 190 words.

5

> **Answers**
> *Informal expressions*:
> Initial greetings: 1, 3
> Congratulations: 1
> Opinion: 2, 5
> Advice/Suggestion: 1, 2, 4, 7
> Linkers: 2, 3, 5, 6, 7
> Endings: 1, 3, 4
> Opening and closing an email / a letter:
> *Hi Brad … Cheers* (informal)
> *Dear Jayne … Love* (informal)
> *Dear Sir … Yours faithfully* (formal; use when the reader's name is not known)
> *Dear Ms Jones … Yours sincerely* (formal)

3 Going places

3.1

Exam skills	Speaking Paper 4 Part 2
	Listening Paper 3 Part 2
	Reading and Use of English Paper 1 Part 1
Vocabulary	Travel and holidays
	Travel collocations and phrasal verbs

3.2

Grammar focus	Modals 1: Obligation, necessity, permission
Exam skills	Reading and Use of English Paper 1 Part 4
Grammar extra	Prepositions of location

Workbook contents

Vocabulary – travel, phrasal verbs, register

Grammar – obligation, necessity, permission; prepositions

3.1 SB pages 22–23

Lesson plan

Speaking	10–15 minutes
Listening	30–40 minutes
Vocabulary	20–25 minutes
SV	Set 7 for homework.
LV	See Extension activity for 3 and 6.

Speaking

1   The aim of this part of the unit is to get the students thinking about the subject of holidays and to find out what vocabulary they already know and what gaps they may have. The photos also act as an introduction to Paper 4 of the examination, when students are each asked to discuss a pair of photos.

Possible answers

Photos 1 and 2

Younger people who like adventure would probably enjoy an activity holiday such as white-water rafting. It's fun to do a sport with other people, because you can make new friends. This type of holiday is never boring. Older people, who want to rest and relax on holiday, might prefer sunbathing on the beach. Some teenagers enjoy a beach holiday because they want to get a good sun tan.

Photos 3 and 4

A backpacking holiday can be fairly cheap and it's a good way of meeting people. Youth hostels are usually in interesting places, often in a central location, and you can

move around an area or country as you please. On the other hand, carrying your rucksack is quite hard work, and youth hostels aren't as comfortable as luxury hotels. In a luxury hotel, everything is done for you, the food is delicious and the hotel has lots of facilities such as a beautiful pool, and this hotel is in a very exotic location. But perhaps it might become boring after a few days? And it will certainly cost a fortune!

Ask students to talk about their own holidays and where they would like to go. This can be broadened into a whole class discussion or kept as pairwork.

Listening

Teaching extra

Any vocabulary should be put up on the board during this part of the lesson, organised into phrases, nouns, verbs (especially phrasal verbs), collocations, etc. This will make it easier for students to get used to organising vocabulary in their notebooks.

2   Before students begin the listening task, brainstorm the vocabulary which they might need. Ask them how many words they can think of under the headings *Ship*, *Trip* and *Weather*. For example:

Ship: to go on a cruise, ship, captain, crew, cabin, deck, passenger, seasickness, a tourist party, to be seasick, on board

Trip: voyage, journey, expedition, to go on holiday

Weather: freezing, icy, wet, stormy, frosty, gales, rough, calm, cold, damp, foggy

Ask students what they know about the Antarctic, and ask them for any words they know connected with it. For example:

iceberg, scientific bases, penguins, to thaw, to melt, to freeze, the polar ice-cap, the South Pole.

1 04 Ask students to read through the questions and try to predict the answers. Play the recording once. The answers are in the order in which they are heard. Students should write down their answers. Play the recording again while students check that their answers are correct.

Tell them that there is *no* need to change the words they hear, i.e. they don't need to make tense changes or change verbs to nouns.

Recording script

Steve: Good morning, everyone. My name is Steve Jackson, and I'm here today to tell you about my recent trip to the Antarctic. Now, the first question people generally ask me, is did I freeze? And my answer is that, amazingly, no, I didn't. The temperature can go as low as minus ten degrees even during the summer months, but while I was there it was about <u>plus seven</u> and I found it quite comfortable. However, you should take warm clothes with you and you really need a windproof coat. But what I found most useful were some <u>sunglasses</u>. The sun can get really strong with the reflection off the snow and ice.

On the ship, I had my own cabin and pretty small it was too. At first I wondered where I was going to put my things, as there was no wardrobe. However, whoever designed the ship thought of just about everything a passenger would need and under the bed there was a <u>cupboard</u>.

The atmosphere on board the ship was great. The crew were mainly American and they really did their best to get everyone to mix. But, of course, you don't have to socialise if you don't want to. The expedition leader was <u>Australian</u>, and he sat at a different table for dinner every night so he'd get to meet us all. He was really friendly and informative.

As to the weather, well, it can get stormy in the Antarctic but the ocean was <u>calm</u> while I was there. That was good, because I was worried about getting sea-sick before I went. Luckily, I was OK, and few of the other passengers had problems.

Do I have any special memories? Well, it's hard to say, really – there are so many. We saw a few whales, especially near a place called Cuverville Island, but I guess what I most treasure is the large variety of <u>birds</u> we saw. They were terrific.

Of course, the Antarctic doesn't have many people living there and the only people we saw, apart from tourists, were a few of the scientists at a <u>research station</u>. They gave us coffee and biscuits one morning! There's a landing strip there, but no harbour or anything like that. You have to get onto shore in a small rubber motorboat.

In the past there used to be a thriving fishing industry in the area, but all that's left are some deserted <u>buildings</u> now. No old boats or machinery or anything like that though.

I'm often asked if I felt guilty about disturbing such an untouched region as Antarctica. I guess, yes, and no. Cruise ships are not allowed to dump <u>rubbish</u> or to go where they like, and they have to take scientists to lead the excursions.

There are rules of course. Only small parties are permitted to land in one area at a time and you've got to keep quiet and not bother the <u>wildlife</u>. So, all in all, I felt that well-run trips, like this one, would do more good than harm. I also felt completely changed by the experience – it was like going to another world. Now, if any of you have any questions …

3 **Round off the listening with a discussion of green tourism / the ethics of tourism.**

Extension activity

This activity can either take five minutes, or, if time and interest allows, can be broadened out into a prepared talk. Divide the class into pairs and explain that each person is going to give a short talk to his/her partner. Allow them each five to ten minutes to prepare a one/two-minute talk on the subject of tourism, A speaking for the subject and B speaking against. Give help with any extra vocabulary that may be needed and then time each speaker exactly. The following are ideas for the talks:
Young people should be encouraged to travel as much as possible.
There are some places in the world which should be protected from tourists.

Vocabulary

4 **Categorising new words into topics will help students remember them. This can be done for any topic. It is a good idea to do the first example, Transport, as a whole-class activity so that students feel comfortable with the exercise.**

Answers
Transport: yacht, coach, ferry, airline
Movement: journey, landing, flight, voyage
Seaside: shore, cliff, coast, harbour
People: backpacker, holiday-makers, crew, travel agent
Accommodation: caravan, campsite, hostel, bed and breakfast

5

Answers
a 7 b 6 c 1 d 8 e 4 f 5 g 3 h 2

Encourage the students to talk about their last holiday in small groups, using the vocabulary they have learned in this unit.

6 Collocations are regularly tested at this level and it is important that students become familiar with verb/noun, verb/adjective, verb/adverb combinations. By asking students if the same words go together in their language, you are making them aware that words collocate differently in different languages.

Answers

take	a trip, a ship, a plane, a flight
book	a trip, a hotel, a flight
catch	a plane, a flight
board	a ship, a plane, a flight
get	a plane, a tan, a hotel, a flight
go	skiing, sightseeing

Extension activity

Students often make mistakes with *holiday, trip, journey, travel, flight, tour, campsite*.

Ask them to correct the mistakes in these sentences.

a For August, I booked a journey to Greece with my wife.
b I hope you will have a good fly.
c For short tours to the shops, I think everyone should ride a bike.
d It would be a good idea to have a travel to Paris.
e I easily got an airplane to Tokyo.
f We stayed at a camping near a lake called Siljan.
g During the journey I did surfing and photography.
h It was early so I went on a trip round the museum.

Answers
a trip b flight c trips d trip e flight
f campsite g trip h tour

7 This task is an easy introduction to Paper 1 Part 1. Ask the students to read through the text and check understanding. The students then have to decide which of A or B is the better answer.

Answers
1 A 2 B 3 B 4 B 5 A 6 B 7 B 8 A

3.2 SB pages 24–25

Lesson plan

Grammar	50–60 minutes
Grammar extra	5–10 minutes

SV Omit 4 and set 6 for homework.
LV See Extension activity for Grammar extra.

Modals 1

1 Check students understand the explanations 1–6. Ask them to give examples of each. For example:

It's forbidden – to smoke in the classroom

It's a good idea – to use an English–English dictionary

All the examples in this exercise are taken from the recording in 3.1. Ask students to discuss which of a–g means 1–6. (There is more than one answer for one.)

Answers
a 6 b 2 c 5 d 3 and 1 e 1 f 4 g 1

2 Let students try to work out the differences between the sentences, but explain the differences if they are finding it difficult. Refer students to the Grammar folder on page 167.

Answers
a The speaker is telling him/herself to do something. (The obligation comes from the speaker.)
b Someone else is telling the speaker what to do. (The obligation doesn't come from the speaker.)
c *Must* is used in laws, notices and rules, where there is no choice of action.
Another point to mention:
Must is often used in a friendly way in conversation, e.g. *You must come to dinner sometime.*

3 This activity is to give free oral practice in using *must, have to* and *don't/didn't have to*. Ask students to look at the example. Then they need to imagine what they would say about transportation, accommodation, food, activities, entertainment and people if they were on a holiday in the places in the pictures.

Refer them to the Grammar folder, page 167, and check they all know that:

the past of *must* is *had to*

must is used in the present tense

have to is used for all other tenses.

Corpus spot

In this exercise students have to correct typical exam candidate errors from the *Cambridge English Corpus*.

4   This gives students more speaking practice using *need, have to, must, should* and *don't have to*, using all tenses. This exercise could be followed up with a writing exercise. Ask students to write five sentences on **a, d** and **f**.

Check that they know that the past of *should do* is *should have done*.

5   Check that students know that *permit* and *allow* are followed by an infinitive with *to*. *Can* and *let* are followed by an infinitive without *to*.

Answers
a   allowed/permitted   b   can   c   let
d   permitted/allowed

Ask students to discuss in pairs the questions about what their parents let them do when they were younger, and what they are allowed to do when they are 18. At the end of the discussion, put up some examples on the board.

Grammar extra

For this exercise students need to visualise where exactly things are. A way to introduce this is to elicit which prepositions might be used in these cases:
1   a line (e.g. a road): on, off, across, along, over
2   a point (e.g. a bus stop): to, from, at
3   an area (e.g. a neighbourhood or park): in, into, out of, across, within, around
4   a volume (e.g. a building): in, into, out of, around
5   a surface (e.g. a table): on, onto, off, over, under, across

Ask students to say where exactly things in the room are, e.g. a picture, a clock, their shoes, a window, their chair, a dress label, etc.

Answers
a   on   b   at   c   into   d   in   e   across   f   in
g   on   h   on   i   into   j   off

Extension activity

Give half the class a map of a small country or island (real or made up), which you have drawn. It will have features such as villages, forests, roads, rivers and mountains. Tell them to keep it hidden. The rest of the class has a map with very few features on it, or completely blank, if you prefer. The aim is for the information about the location of the features to be transferred only by speaking and listening. The student with the completed map tells the one with the blank map exactly where everything is positioned, and the student draws in the features on their map. Pointing isn't allowed!

6   This is examination practice for Paper 1 Part 4. Refer students to the Exam spot. Check that they know that they cannot change the word given and that they shouldn't use more than five words. Contractions are counted as two words. Normally there are only six questions, but you have eight here to give more practice.

Answers
1   had to change
2   is forbidden to smoke
3   did not / didn't let me go
4   are not / aren't permitted to swim
5   should get health insurance
6   do not / don't have to wear / do not / don't need to have
7   do not / don't need to put
8   have got to ring/phone

Exam folder 2

SB pages 26–27

Paper 1 Part 3
Word formation

Explain that the word formation task is the third part of the Reading and Use of English paper. The whole paper takes 1 hour and 15 minutes to do and students should aim to spend about 10–12 minutes on this part. This may seem to them too short a time at first, so stress that they will become faster with practice. There are eight questions in this part of the paper. Students should be encouraged to read through the whole passage before they start trying to do the answers.

1   Introduce the idea that words can be made negative by putting a prefix at the beginning.

Try to elicit some examples to put on the board before students do the task. Notice that *il-* is usually in front of words beginning with *l* and *ir-* in front of words beginning with *r*. *Im-* is often before words beginning with *p*, but not always.

Answers
a	dis-	dissatisfied	h	un-	unhappy
b	im-	impatient	i	ir-	irresponsible
c	in-	inexpensive	j	mis-	misunderstand
d	il-	illegal	k	dis-	disappear
e	im-	impossible	l	ir-	irregular
f	un-	uncomfortable	m	im-	immoral
g	dis-	dishonest			

2   Not all prefixes are negative. Ask students what they think *non-*, *re-*, *sub-*, *un-* and *under-* mean.

Answers
a   without stopping: *non-* = not, e.g. *non-smoker, non-stick*
b   to train again: *re-* = again, e.g. *re-grow, replace, redo*
c   *a path/passage* under the road: *sub-* = under, e.g. *submarine, subtotal, substandard*
d   undo an action: *un-* = reverse an action, e.g. *unlock, unfasten*
e   put a line underneath / emphasise something: *under-* = below or not enough, e.g. *underwater, underfed, underwatered, undervalue*

It is very useful for the students to realise that they can enlarge their vocabularies by learning how a word can be changed into a noun, adjective, verb or adverb. There are no rules which are easily accessible to students at this level (the suffix often depends on the origin of the word – Latin, Anglo-Saxon, Greek, etc.) and therefore they just need to learn them.

3

Answers
a	happiness	b	intelligence	c	approval
d	recommendation	e	action	f	popularity
g	friendship	h	payment	i	tourist/tourism

4

Answers
a	truth	b	success	c	death	d	height

5

Answers
a	windy	b	attractive	c	hopeful/hopeless
d	dangerous	e	endless	f	accidental
g	valuable	h	accessible		

6   Normally we change an adjective into an adverb by adding *-ly*.
Words ending in *-y* – the *y* usually changes to *i* + *-ly*.
Words ending in *-le* – change *le* to *ly* after a consonant.
Adjectives ending in *-ic* – add *-ally*.

Answers
a	steadily	b	actively	c	necessarily	d	annually
e	extraordinarily	f	automatically				

7

Answers
a	renew	h	communication
b	discourage	i	measurement
c	undo, redo	j	satisfaction, dissatisfaction
d	rebuild	k	maintenance
e	repay	l	identification
f	disapprove	m	introduction
g	unlock, relock	n	criticism

8   Read through the Advice box and check that students have understood what they have to do. If time is short, then this exercise can be set for homework, otherwise it can be done in pairs or individually in the class. Tell students to always look carefully for prefixes, especially negative ones, and plurals.

Answers
1	verb – PRODUCED	5	noun – SAFETY
2	noun – YOUTH	6	noun – REPRESENTATIVE
3	adverb – EXTREMELY	7	noun – APPEARANCE
4	adjective – SCIENTIFIC	8	adjective – IMPOSSIBLE

4.1

Speaking	
Exam skills	Reading and Use of English Paper 1 Part 7
Vocabulary	Word formation

4.2

Grammar focus	*as* and *like*
	Compound adjectives
Exam skills	Reading and Use of English Paper 1 Part 4
Vocabulary	Topic set – parts of animals
	Expressions with *time*

Workbook contents

Reading – guessing unknown words
Listening Paper 3 Part 2 – sentence completion
Grammar – *as* and *like*, compound adjectives

4.1 SB pages 28–29

Lesson plan

Reading	50–60 minutes
Vocabulary	10–20 minutes

SV	Set 6 for homework.
LV	See Extension activity in 6.

Reading

Answers
1 polar bear   2 thick-billed parrot   3 tiger shark
4 snow leopard   5 koala   6 orang-utan

All the animals are endangered except for the tiger shark. The snow leopard is endangered because of hunting; the polar bear from global warming; the orang-utan, thick-billed parrot and koala because of habitat destruction.

1 Ask the students to match the correct animal or bird with the correct photo.

In pairs or groups, ask the class to discuss which animal they would save if they could choose. They should give reasons for their choice.

2 Make sure the students have access to English–English dictionaries. They must work in pairs or alone to match a–e with 1–5.

Answers
a 3   b 1   c 4   d 2   e 5

3 Students skim the texts to say where they come from. At this stage there might be some discussion about the different genres, i.e. what differences there are between a magazine article, an encyclopaedia, a brochure and a novel.

Answer
c   an article

4 Refer the students to the Exam spot.

Students now scan the texts to find the information. Tell the students not to worry about individual words that they don't know. Don't let them use a translation dictionary during this exercise. Questions a and b give practice in the type of scanning the students need to do and raise their awareness of distractors in the texts (words that might at first seem to give the answers, but in fact do not).

Answers
b D

1 C   2 A   3 B   4 A   5 D   6 E
7 E   8 B   9 E   10 C

5 Ask the students to talk about the questions either in pairs or groups.

Vocabulary

6

Answers
a traditional   b endangered   c decision
d visitors   e conservation   f entrance
g zoology   h sights   i unhappy   j rainfall

Extension activity

Choose more words from the texts and put their base words on the board, in the same way as the words in exercise 6. Get the students to look through the texts to find the words.

4.2 SB pages 30–31

Lesson plan

Grammar	30–40 minutes
Vocabulary	25–35 minutes

SV   Set 5 and 6 for homework.
LV   See Extension activity for 5.

as and *like*

1   Ask the class to look at the examples and refer them to the Corpus spot and the Grammar folder, page 167.

2   Ask the class to complete the sentences, using *as*, *like* or nothing (–), as appropriate.

Answers
a like   b –   c –   d like   e like   f as   g as

3

Answers
1   described in the brochure as
2   use the garage as/for storage
3   was working as a teacher
4   is usually known as
5   what sounded like
6   refer to my dog as

Compound adjectives

4   Compound adjectives are very useful when writing descriptions, both of people and things. It is also important that students learn to recognise them when they come across them in their reading.

Answers
a   1   animals in general
    2   a tiger which eats people (not just men!)
    3   a blue-eyed, long-haired, bad-tempered cat
c   1   You would sit in a car.
    2   If you are hard-up, you don't have much money, so you may not be very happy.
    3   You need to have a lot of money.
        More examples of this type are: a phone-in programme, a pick-up truck, a standby flight, a takeaway meal
d   1   a fifty-kilometre road
    2   a twelve-year-old girl
    3   a seventy-five-minute film
    4   a thirty-five-thousand-pound car
    5   a ten-second pause

Vocabulary

5   If time is short, this exercise can be set for homework. It can also be used for dictionary work, using an English–English dictionary.

Answers
parrot – beak, feathers, wing, tail
bear – fur, paw, tail
tiger – fur, paw, tail
rhino – horn, tail

Tell students to think of an animal and give them a minute to decide how to describe it so that their partner can guess what it is. For example:

It's a grey-skinned, large-footed, big-eared and short-tailed animal who lives in Africa and India.

(Answer: an elephant)

Extension activity

There are many expressions in English where comparisons are made with animals, e.g. *as quiet as a mouse*.

It is often a good idea to introduce these expressions by asking students what they think things are compared to in English. For example: *as hot as? as cold as? as hungry as? as drunk as?* They will probably say a variety of things and be amused to find out some of the answers (*as hot as hell, as cold as ice, as hungry as a hunter, as drunk as a lord*). Students often find it interesting to compare what they would say in their own language, with the English saying.

Examples with animals are:
as brave as a lion
as strong as an ox
as slippery as an eel
as stubborn as a mule
as poor as a church mouse

6   Go through the expressions, explaining what they mean and how you'd use them. Give some examples for each one. Try to make the examples relevant to the students. For example:

This morning I spent a long time in a traffic jam on my way to class.

How much time do you spend doing homework?

What do you do to pass the time when you are on holiday?

This exercise can be set for homework, if time is short.

Answers

a	one at a time	e	have a good time
b	time for breakfast	f	kill time / pass the time
c	times as much	g	tell the time
d	In time	h	wasting time / spending time

7   Ask students to discuss the questions in pairs.

Writing folder 2

SB pages 32–33

Paper 2 Part 1 Essays

Refer students to the information about Part 1 at the top of the page and stress that they must answer this question in the exam. They need to read the question carefully to understand what content points they have to include – the third point is their own and it must be relevant to the task set.

1   Ask students to read the question and elicit their ideas for a possible third content point. Then ask them to read the sample answer and decide which point the writer has omitted. Refer them to the information under Assessment focus.

Answers
Although mentioned in the introduction, point 2 – wildlife under threat – is missing.

2   Suggest students work in pairs and decide together where the linking phrases should be inserted.

Sample answer
(with phrases inserted in bold)

THE TREATMENT OF ANIMALS IN OUR WORLD TODAY

This is a complex question. Many people depend on animals to live, whether they eat meat or just keep an animal for its milk. This essay will consider farming, **as well as discussing** the role of zoos and endangered wildlife.

When zoos first opened, they had a real purpose – to educate people. There was no television and **in this way** people got to see animals from other places. Now we don't have the same need for zoos and it is cruel to lock animals up there. **For this reason**, I think all zoos should be closed.

As for agriculture, I think some farmers look after animals well, but many don't care about the conditions that their animals live in. The best farmers give animals plenty of space and fresh grass to eat.

To sum up, I think we could treat animals better.

3   Ask students to write a paragraph, and go round monitoring their work.

Sample paragraph
In terms of endangered wildlife, man is often to blame for the disappearance of species. Pollution from factories and cars causes severe problems. Some chemicals are being released into the environment which are harmful to bees, for example.

4   Explain that the repetition of basic words is to be avoided, as it will make a negative impression on the examiner. Elicit answers (reworked answer is given in 6 below).

5

Answers
See reworked essay below.
Phrase b doesn't fit grammatically.

6   Tell students to avoid single sentence paragraphs in their writing.

Reworked essay
(includes new paragraph in 3, phrases in 5 and final sentence in 6)

THE TREATMENT OF ANIMALS IN OUR WORLD TODAY

This is a complex question. Many people depend on animals to live, whether they eat meat or just keep **a cow or a goat** for its milk. This essay will consider farming, as well as discussing the role of zoos and endangered wildlife.

When zoos first opened, they had a real purpose – to educate people. There was no television and in this way people got to see **wildlife** from other places. Now we don't have the same need for zoos and it is cruel to lock **creatures** up there. For this reason, all zoos should be closed *in my opinion*.

In terms of endangered wildlife, man is often to blame for the disappearance of species. Pollution from factories and cars causes severe problems. Some chemicals are being released into the environment, which are harmful to bees, for example.

As for agriculture, *it is true that* some farmers look after animals well, but many don't care about the conditions that **they** live in. The best farmers give **them** plenty of space and fresh grass to eat.

To sum up, we could treat animals better *without a doubt*. **We need to respect all living creatures.**

7   **Set the essay for homework.**

Sample answer

WILDLIFE IN NEED OF PROTECTION

As the statement suggests, there are many species at risk today. This essay will give some examples of endangered animals, argue for their better protection and explain what action could be taken now.

Arctic animals, such as polar bears, are in danger of extinction due to global warming. Other species, such as the white rhino, are facing extinction because they are hunted.

If we let these beautiful creatures disappear, our world will never be the same. Think of a forest without any birds singing or an ocean with no whales. Furthermore, when species die out, the whole balance of nature is threatened.

So what is to be done? There are already several protection programmes but these often lack money. It is also necessary for governments to pass additional environmental laws, in my opinion, so that the pollution from factories can be better controlled.

In conclusion, there is no doubt that more could be done to save endangered species. They are worth saving so that future generations can admire them.

(174 words)

5 Mixed emotions

5.1

Exam skills	Skills for Listening
Vocabulary	Collocations – adverbs of degree with adjectives of feeling
Grammar extra	Irregular verbs

5.2

Grammar focus	Review of past tenses
Exam skills	Reading and Use of English, Paper 1 Part 2

Workbook contents

Vocabulary – letter of complaint
Grammar – past tenses
Reading and Use of English Paper 1 Part 7 – multiple matching

5.1 SB pages 34–35

Lesson plan

Speaking	10–20 minutes
Vocabulary	15–20 minutes
Listening	30–40 minutes
Grammar extra	5–10 minutes

SV   Shorten speaking in 2; set Grammar extra table for homework.

LV   Use the Extension activity after 5 to work on the pronunciation of past tense endings.

1   Students group the adjectives according to whether they describe positive or negative emotions. If time permits, ask them to pair up adjectives with similar meaning.

Answers
positive: content, delighted, happy, pleased, satisfied, thrilled (content = satisfied, happy = pleased, delighted = thrilled)
negative: anxious, frightened, petrified, scared, tense, terrified, uneasy, worried (anxious = worried, frightened = scared, petrified = terrified, tense = uneasy)
Scared and *worried* combine with *stiff* (as does *bored*). Explain that *scared stiff* means extremely scared.

2   Give students 3–5 minutes to discuss in pairs and then elicit reactions to what is shown in the pictures. Remind them to use some of the descriptive language given in exercise 1. Ask what else students find frightening, and what other situations make them feel happy. This can be omitted if time is short.

Vocabulary

3   Elicit answers and students' ideas as to why some adjectives combine with adverbs like *absolutely*, while others are only used with adverbs like *very*. Explain that all six adverbs in the box in 4 are adverbs of degree, which are used to indicate the extent of something – in this case, the strength of an emotion. Adverbs like *absolutely*, *completely*, *totally* are examples of emphasising adverbs which are used with adjectives to strengthen or emphasise the meaning to the extent of 100% the adjective described. They are used with adjectives whose meaning already suggests extreme feeling or size, such as *terrified*. Remind students that we cannot say 'very terrified' or 'a little terrified'. Adverbs of degree like *very*, *extremely*, *really* also strengthen the meaning, but only to the extent of 'a lot', rather than 100%. We can say 'very frightened' and also 'a little frightened'. Another adverb of this type at B2 level is *entirely*.

Answers
In **a**, the first sentence is correct. (*very* happy = a lot)
In **b**, the second sentence is correct. (*absolutely* delighted = 100%)

4   Refer students to the Corpus spot, then ask them to complete the sentences and elicit answers.

Answers
absolutely, *completely* and *totally* can be used in **a** and **d**; *extremely*, *really* and *very* can be used in **b**, **c**, **e** and **f**.

Listening

5   **1 05** Explain that students will hear many of the adjectives and adverbs in the recordings which follow. Play the recording once and check students are able to answer the two gist questions: where the man was and how long he spent there.

Answers
The man was in a lift.
He spent over four hours there.

Recording script

1

I'd had this interview for a job, up on the twenty-seventh floor of a big office block. It was after six and a lot of people had already left. I got in the lift and pressed the button. At first, I noticed that it sort of shook but it started to go down. Then there was this horrible sound of twisting metal and it shuddered to a stop. I was stuck between the twelfth and thirteenth floors! To begin with, I was determined not to panic. There was an emergency button, which I pushed for ages. Next, I saw a phone, but when I lifted the receiver, it was dead. At this point, I completely went to pieces. I shouted and screamed, I hammered on the doors, but nobody helped. Eventually, I sank to the floor and wept like a child. In the end, it was a good four hours before the night porter realised what had happened and called the Fire Brigade. I've never been in one since.

Play the recording again and ask students to take it in turns to narrate what happened. The answers to the questions give the basic storyline.

Answers
1 to attend an interview for a job
2 early evening
3 He tried to press the emergency button and use the phone.
4 Most people had already left and it was four hours before the night porter realised he was there.

Extension activity

In the extract, there are a number of verbs with regular past tense endings. Although the spelling of these is always -ed, the pronunciation varies. Get students to listen to the extract again and write down the verbs which contain the /ɪd/ sound. Elicit when this happens.

Answers
started   lifted   shouted
The /ɪd/ ending follows the consonants *t* and *d*.

6 **1 05** ◄ Ask students to look at the question for the extract they have just heard. Play the recording again, asking them to note down sequence words and phrases. The question here and those in 7 are similar to the type you find in Listening Part 1, but the recordings are longer and not typical of the exam. This is to give students more context for identifying their answers, and also to focus on narrative and past tenses.

Answer
1 C The phrase *to begin with* signals the answer. Other sequence words and phrases are: *at first, then, next, at this point, eventually, in the end.*

7 **1 06** Ask students to read through questions 2–8, thinking about the words in bold. Then play the recording straight through. Each extract will be heard twice. Remind students to check their answers at the second listening.

Answers
2 B   3 C   4 C   5 A   6 B   7 A   8 B

Recording script

2

Somehow I have to sort out their problem, this fear they have of flying. First, we talk as a group, and one by one they tell me about particular times when they've flown and what happened. Nine times out of ten they describe regular, problem-free flights, just like the hundreds I flew myself. You see, most of their worries are only in their imagination. I also use drama and role play to teach them how to deal with other people's fears, because through that they sometimes forget their own problem, or take it less seriously than before. Finally, but only if I think it's still necessary, we go up in a plane. My passenger is accompanied by an actor, who plays the part of the nervous first-time traveller. I sit a few rows behind and it's wonderful to watch my 'student' staying calm, offering advice to this stranger. I've never failed yet.

3

On the phone

Son: Mum, it's me. Look, I know you must be really angry and I'm very sorry, we didn't mean to get lost out on the hills, but …

Woman: Oh Tom, it's so good to hear your voice! We've been worried stiff since the police called round – we were sure this phone call would be bad news. I mean, it's been three days! Are you really OK?

Son: Yeah. Helen's got a few bruises from her fall, and we haven't eaten much in three days obviously, but other than that, yeah, we're doing fine.

Woman: Well, that's something. Your dad is still absolutely furious with you, of course. When do you think you'll be able to get home?

Son: The day after tomorrow, all being well. We …

4

It was late at night and I was in the living room watching television on my own. Funnily enough, I was watching a horror movie – it wasn't very scary though! Well, I thought I heard a noise upstairs. So I turned off the TV, held my breath and listened. And then, there was this horrific crash. My first thought was – it's a burglar. I was scared stiff but I knew I had to go up there. I remember I picked up an umbrella – goodness knows what I would have done with it! Anyway, I crept up the stairs and the first thing I saw was a bookcase on its side, with hundreds of books on the floor. Then I heard this whimpering sound, coming from underneath the pile of books. It was the next-door neighbour's cat I'd heard! While I was putting away the books, I found something else. <u>A live frog! That's when I was absolutely petrified!</u> It sort of jumped out at me.

5

Hi, Julie. If your phone's switched off, I guess you must be celebrating! Wow! This must feel as good as the day you graduated from university! No, even better than that! Anyway, just to say you've made me a very proud dad! I'm absolutely delighted for you. You've worked so hard to achieve your goal and you thoroughly deserve what they've offered you. <u>I can't wait to see your novel in the shops</u> – when will it be coming out, do you know? It's funny, isn't it, all those writing competitions you went in for as a child and you never won a thing, but you never gave up, did you? Well, as I said, I am really, really proud of you. Speak soon. Love you.

6

We were all living in a small house in the countryside at the time. The house was in the middle of nowhere and it was quite a long journey back from the university each evening, so I'd bought myself a small motorbike. Anyway, on one particular evening I was on my way home when a really thick fog came down. I didn't know where I was and I became very uneasy. I went on – rather slowly – but couldn't see anything I recognised. At one point the road curved round, but because of the fog I didn't see this and carried straight on … and hit a wall. The impact threw me off the bike and I ended up underneath it, with my leg trapped. I screamed for help but of course there was no one about. I realised that I had to get up and carry on – or stay there all night. So I pulled myself out from under the bike, got back on and somehow arrived home, where my friends all took one look at me and <u>called an ambulance</u>. I needed seven stitches and they kept me in for observation.

7

Interviewer: Malcolm Jarvis, you have recently sailed single-handedly around the world. At one stage, you were shipwrecked all alone in the middle of the ocean, clinging on to your damaged yacht. Weren't you terrified?

MJ: Not at the time. I suppose I was too busy trying to survive.

Interviewer: You mean finding things to eat?

MJ: More basic than hunger! First, I had to get myself out of the sea. Sharks had been a problem there. I managed to pull myself back into the yacht but it had taken in a lot of water. So I spent a bit of time sorting that out.

Interviewer: And then were you able to keep yourself warm?

MJ: Only for a while. I wrapped myself in whatever I could find, including the sails, but by the second day I was in a really bad way because <u>I couldn't feel my fingers and toes, they were completely numb. That was the most dreadful time.</u> It was just as well they found me when they did.

8

We were all in the main room planning what to do that day. The others were looking at a map on the table, but I was standing by the back window. About six of them burst in, waving guns and shouting things in a dialect we didn't understand. I <u>knew they hadn't seen me</u> over by the open window. They grabbed John and Gary. Ruth rushed to the doorway but they got her too. In the meantime, <u>I had managed to throw myself safely outside</u> and had crawled underneath the house – because of the rainy season, all the houses there are raised above the ground on wooden stilts. I kept totally still. I remember watching a beetle on a leaf, staring at it and hoping that they wouldn't find me. Finally, when I realised that they'd gone, I ran inside and radioed for help. My friends weren't so lucky. They were held as hostages for over three months.

8   Extract 8 contextualises the use of the past perfect. After getting students to note down the order of events, ask them to check their notes by listening to the recording, paying attention to when this tense is used.

Grammar extra

If this is set for homework, remind students to think about other verbs which have the same form throughout.

> **Answers**
> The verb forms appear on page 168 of the Grammar folder.
> *Burst* has the same form. Other verbs like this are, for example, *cut, hit, set, put, bet.*

Teaching extra

To encourage students to write short pieces of narration on a regular basis, start a class ring-binder file called 'True stories'. Ask students to include funny, frightening or other unusual personal accounts, and suggest that others in the class read these. You could even state that the stories can be fact or fiction, with the class deciding whether the writer has made up the story or not.

5.2 SB pages 36–37

Lesson plan	
Grammar	60–70 minutes
Use of English	10–20 minutes

SV Set 4 as a written task for homework; shorten the work on parts of speech in 6.

LV Ask students to write up their descriptions of the action story in 4 in class.

Review of past tenses

1   Ask students to work through the examples on their own and then compare answers with a partner.

Answers
a PP   **b** PS; PS   **c** P   **d** PC   **e** PS; PP   **f** PC; PS
g PC; PC   **h** PS; PP   **i** PS; PP; PS   **j** P

Elicit the reasons why two different tenses are used in **e**, **h** and **i**.

Answer
In the sentences where the past simple and past perfect are used, the past perfect refers to an action further back in the past.

Now ask students to think about the different tenses used in **f**. They should then read the explanation about the past simple and past continuous, which follows in the Student's Book.

2   Ask students to fill in the gaps, using either the past simple or past continuous. They can then compare their answers.

Answers

1	was walking	15	drew
2	was blowing	16	pulled away
3	was pouring	17	was
4	was	18	stood
5	drove	19	was coming down
6	stopped	20	was shaking
7	curved	21	(was) wondering
8	decided	22	came
9	was feeling	23	was pushing
10	got	24	grabbed
11	drove	25	made
12	happened	26	went
13	pulled up	27	was trying
14	waited	28	heard

3   Ask students to look at the information about the past simple and past perfect. They can then complete the sentences.

Answers
a had spent; got
b told; had happened; explained; had found
c had kept; thought; was

4   Ask students to work in pairs, taking it in turns to describe each scene, starting with the fourth one and working backwards.

Useful vocabulary
Picture 1: hold up a bank, a hold-up / a bank raid, masked robbers, balaclava, pointing a gun at / at gunpoint, cashier
Picture 2: make a getaway, drive off, bag/holdall
Picture 3: car chase, police siren, catch up with
Picture 4: force to stop, pull over, arrest, take off (the balaclavas)

Background information
Raymond Chandler, author of *The Big Sleep*, was born in Chicago, but went to school in London. For most of his life, he lived in Southern California, which is where most of his novels are set. His most famous character is the private detective Philip Marlowe, who has been played in films by Humphrey Bogart, Robert Mitchum and Elliot Gould.

5   Ask students to read the extract and decide why the narrator wasn't frightened.

6   Explain that this task is an introduction to the 'open cloze', Paper 1 Part 2, which tests mainly grammar. Ask students to work through the gaps in pairs and then check their answers with another pair of students.

Answers
1 at   **2** the   **3** when   **4** of   **5** and   **6** any
7 had   **8** so   **9** not   **10** was   **11** it   **12** went

Write the following headings on the board and ask students to sort the words into these categories.

ADVERBS   CONJUNCTIONS   DETERMINERS
PREPOSITIONS   PRONOUNS   QUANTIFIERS   VERBS

Answers
adverb: not
determiner: the
conjunctions: and, because, so, when
prepositions: at, of
pronoun: it
quantifiers: any, some
verbs: be, had, has, was, went

Remind students that these types of words are commonly tested in this part of Paper 1. Exam folder 3 on the following two pages of the Student's Book covers Paper 1 Part 2.

Exam folder 3

Paper 1 Part 2 Open cloze

The open cloze consists of eight gaps and an example at the beginning. Each gap can only be filled with one word – you can't use contractions. If students put in more than one word, the answer will be marked wrong. The word must be spelt correctly. The gaps are mainly grammatical in focus, but there are sometimes one or two vocabulary items in the form of a collocation or phrasal verb.

Teaching extra

If your students need to gain confidence, this type of gapped task can be introduced gradually, starting at sentence level. Give students sentences with words blanked out. Each block of sentences could deal with one grammatical area – determiners, prepositions, relative pronouns, quantifiers, etc. When more confident, the students can work through a whole passage. The first passage could gap prepositions only. Continue in this way with determiners, quantifiers, relative pronouns, conjunctions and so on, until the students know what to look for. Later they can move on to a mixed open cloze passage.

1

Answers
a few
b keep
c the
d must
e been
f up
g himself
h who
i many
j unless
k to

2 Students need to get used to using all the clues they are given. The title is obviously a good clue. Make sure they read the whole passage before they attempt to answer this question.

Answer
'Balancing the risks' is the best title, as the text looks at both sides of the question.

3

Answers
1 SPEND
2 UNLESS
3 A
4 FEW
5 IF/THOUGH
6 THAN
7 IN
8 SUCH

6 What if?

Topic Winning prizes and celebrity culture

6.1

Exam skills	Reading and Use of English Paper 1 Parts 3 and 6
Vocabulary	Phrasal verbs with *keep*

6.2

Listening	(non-exam, listening to authentic speech)
Grammar focus	Conditionals with *if* and *unless*
Exam skills	Reading and Use of English Paper 1 Part 1
	Speaking Paper 4 Part 4

Workbook contents

Listening Paper 3 Part 1 – short extracts
Grammar – conditionals with *if* and *unless*
Reading and Use of English Paper 1 Part 4 – key word transformations
Vocabulary – parts of speech
Writing – word order and punctuation

6.1 SB pages 40–41

Lesson plan	
Reading	40–50 minutes
Vocabulary	30–40 minutes
SV	Keep warmer discussion in 1 brief. Set 8 for homework.
LV	See Extenstion activity after 7.

Reading

1 Allow students a few minutes to discuss their ideas in pairs. Summarise the advantages and drawbacks on the board.

2 Encourage students to skim headlines and opening paragraphs to discover gist meaning.

> **Answer**
> The girl, Mary-Jess Leaverland, appeared on a regional TV talent show in China.

3 Refer students to the Exam spot and ask them to read the whole text, thinking about the content suggested by the parts in red. Check understanding of these phrases.

4 Ask students to work individually and compare answers in pairs.

> **Answers**
> **1** G   **2** F   **3** D   **4** A   **5** B   **6** E
> The extra sentence is C.

5 Elicit students' ideas. For a fuller discussion, ask students to think of other instant celebrities and how their lives have changed for the better or worse.

Vocabulary

6 Refer to the example from the text (**keep on**). This phrasal verb is very common and is easy to understand because the particle (**on**) doesn't alter the meaning of the main verb – the sentence *People keep stopping her in the street* would mean the same. Ask students to match the phrasal verbs to their definitions and elicit their answers. Suggest they think about the particles as they do this – for example, 'down' might be to do with position, movement or direction.

> **Answers**
> **a** keep down   **b** keep in   **c** keep up with
> **d** keep to   **e** keep up with   **f** keep away

7 Ask students to complete the exercise in pairs. Explain that the number of words indicated by the gaps shows them whether a pronoun is needed.

> **Answers**
> **a** kept to   **b** kept up with   **c** keep away
> **d** keep up with her   **e** keeping him in   **f** keep to
> **g** keeps to   **h** keeps on; keep it down

> **E**xtension activity
>
> Point out the use of the adverbs *rarely* and *generally* in 7 b and c. Write these other adverbs of frequency on the board – *frequently, occasionally, regularly, seldom* – and check students understand them. Ask students to include them in the following sentences and complete the sentences in their own words. Sentence **b** should contain two adverbs.
> **a** At the weekend, I get up late because …
> **b** When I was younger I played computer games but now …
> **c** I forget people's names at parties so …

8 Ask students to skim the text for its general meaning. Check understanding of the words 1–8 in capitals. Suggest students think about the words around each gap to work out what part of speech is needed. Refer them back to Exam folder 2 for further advice on this exam task.

Answers
1 impossible   **2** argument   **3** living   **4** endlessly
5 personal   **6** understandable   **7** scientists
8 hunters

6.2 SB pages 42–43

Lesson plan

Listening	10–20 minutes
Grammar focus	30–40 minutes
Exam skills	15 minutes
Speaking	10–15 minutes

SV   Set 7 and 8 for homework.
LV   See Extension activity for 1. Extend discussion in 9.

Conditionals with *if*

1 1 07 **Explain that students are going to hear four British people talking for less than a minute each. There will be some unfamiliar words and phrases, but students should not be put off by this. For each speaker, they should concentrate on listening for the answer to the focus question (How would their lives change if they won the lottery?). Point out to students that each speaker will use the second conditional form, at least in part (*I'd …*). This will cue the answers for them.**

After eliciting answers, point out the speakers' use of phrasal verbs in extracts 2, 3 and 4:

extract 2   *stand out* – here, the meaning is 'be better' (students also met this phrasal verb in 1.1, meaning 'easy to see')

extracts 3 and 4   *sort out* – here, the meaning is 'solve (a problem)'; another meaning of this phrasal verb is 'tidy'

Suggested answers
Speaker 1 would buy a new car and a new house. He'd also buy a house in Spain and a flat in Manhattan. He'd employ a chef and a masseur.

Speaker 2 would buy a yacht and hire a crew and chef and sail around the world.

Speaker 3 would pay off her and her family's debts. Then she would buy a huge house in the country and invite friends

and people who didn't usually have the opportunity to visit the countryside.

Speaker 4 would also pay off his and his family's debts. Then he would invest the rest of the money and live off the interest. He'd move from Britain to a warmer country.

Recording script

1
I'd buy a Seychelles blue Bentley convertible. I'd buy a nice fat house in Holland Park. I'd get a lovely big house in the countryside. I'd buy a beautiful house in Spain, with swimming pool, palm trees, that sort of thing. I'd get a flat in Manhattan probably. Um … I'd also have a permanent chef … top of the range chef who could cook all different types of food, so I could have whatever food I wanted whenever I wanted it. I'd have my own personal masseur …

2
I think I would just alter my life entirely. I love the sun, and a Caribbean holiday stands out in my memory … surrounded by clear turquoise sea … so I think I'd buy a yacht. And as I don't know anything about um … sailing, I'd have to buy a crew as well. So, um, I'd get … I'd get this luxurious yacht and a very skilled crew – and probably a skilled cook – who would just take me all around the world going from hot spot to hot spot, so I could have a really great time.

3
Well, I know I'd have a problem with having all that money. I'd … I think it is a problem really, in some ways, because you … you'd have a sort of social responsibility and there are all kinds of people who you need to help, which I would want to do very much. Um, so of course I'd sort out my debts, my family's, but in the end I think what I'd do is buy – depending on how much money I had – buy a huge house, a really massive house somewhere in the country and just surround myself by all the people I want to be with, um and people who perhaps never had a chance to get out into the country at all.

4
Again depending on how many millions I won, um it would change what I would or wouldn't do with it. Frankly, if it was a lot, I mean five million upwards … sort out my own debts, which God knows are bad enough, sort out the family's debts and then invest as much as possible and just try and live off the interest, keep it there, nice little nest egg, growing and growing and growing, developing, flowering bountifully, and holiday, get away, move, anywhere but cold Britain.

Extension activity

Ask students to listen again and note down any words or phrases they hear related to the following:
Speaker 1 – an exclusive lifestyle
Speaker 2 – sailing
Speaker 3 – problems
Speaker 4 – money

Answers
Speaker 1: Bentley convertible, top of the range, permanent chef, personal masseur
Speaker 2: luxurious yacht, skilled crew, going from hot spot to hot spot
Speaker 3: social responsibility, sort out debts, people who never had a chance
Speaker 4: £5 million upwards, debts, invest, live off the interest, a nest egg

As a short follow-up writing task for homework, students could then use some of this language, writing a paragraph about one of the four speakers.

Suggested answer
If Speaker 4 won a large sum of money on the lottery, first of all, he would sort out his and his family's debts, then he would invest the rest of the money and live off the interest. He talks about having a nest egg, which would grow, and which he could use to travel.

2 Most students will already have been taught most conditional forms at an earlier stage, but may need to be reminded of the second and third conditionals. Elicit the full forms of the contracted verbs and the conditional types. Refer students to the Grammar folder if necessary.

Answers
a I would (type 2 conditional)
b had not won … would not have been able (type 3 conditional)

3 Students can complete the matching exercise in pairs.

Answers
a 4   b 1   c 7   d 2   e 6   f 3   g 8   h 5

Conditionals with *unless*

4 Refer students to the examples. Explain that *unless* can be seen as meaning *if not*, e.g:
a … if Juan doesn't arrive soon
b If you haven't already got tickets …

Corpus spot

Answers
a There will be no improvement in my tennis unless I ~~don't~~ get some training.
b *correct*
c People hardly ever use candlelight today unless there ~~isn't anything~~ **is something** wrong with the power supply.
d There isn't much to do in the city unless you **have** (**got**) friends.
e You must stop working so hard **if you don't want to** end up in hospital sooner or later.
f *correct*

5

Answers
Tense errors
won't → wouldn't (be so unreliable)
hasn't → hadn't (run out of)
I'll find → I find
can't → couldn't (i.e. couldn't call)
will say → would say OR didn't get → don't get
will get → gets (really angry)
will do → do (the journey)

1 unless   2 If   3 if   4 if   5 unless   6 if
7 If   8 if   9 unless

6 Ask students to spend a couple of minutes finishing the sentences in pairs. Then ask pairs to report back to the whole class. Correct any errors in conditional forms. Write up some examples on the board and at the end ask students to identify them again.

7 Refer students to the Exam spot on Paper 1 Part 1. Elicit other parts of speech, such as adverbs, pronouns, conjunctions. Then ask students in pairs to sort the words into the four categories. Remind them that some words may fit into more than one category, so they will have to check that the meaning of each group of four words is similar.

Answers
Nouns: attempt, experiment, trial, try
Verbs: accepted, gathered, received, welcomed
Prepositions: by, in, on, to
Adjectives: delicate, gentle, light, tiny

8 Students complete the short article, using one option from each group of words.

Answers
1 attempt   2 light   3 received   4 by

If there is enough time, ask students to discuss their views on the story. What is the 'fuss' that the elderly woman referred to? (Publicity.) Why did she not want to claim her jackpot prize? (The excitement and media attention might kill her.)

DO YOU WANT TO CHECK STUDENT PROGRESS?
PROGRESS TEST 3 ON THE TEACHER'S RESOURCES CD-ROM

Speaking

9 Refer students to the useful language and ask them to discuss the questions in pairs or groups for 3–5 minutes. Then elicit ideas from the class, encouraging use of the phrases given.

Writing folder 3

SB pages 44–45

Paper 2 Part 2 Reports

Refer students to the information at the top of the page and elicit their views on what register a report should be written in. This will depend slightly on who the end reader of the report is, but generally, a report should be formal.

1 Ask students to read the exam question and sample answer. Elicit their views on the usefulness of the information given.

Answers
Yes, the report contains useful information. It states what is wrong with the museum and makes recommendations.

2 Suggest students match the headings individually and then compare their answers in pairs.

Answers
1 F   2 D   3 C   4 A   5 B

3 Refer students to the information in the Assessment focus and encourage them to use as wide a range of structures and vocabulary as possible. This will help them to get a high mark for their writing in the exam.

Answers
Conditional structures:
Paragraph 3: This permanent exhibition will remain unappealing to visitors *unless* it is updated.
Paragraph 5: Wademouth Museum would have a brighter future *if* its displays were improved.
a if   E
b Unless G
c if   G
d if   E
e unless G

4 If time is short, divide the class in two and get students in each half to write one of the paragraphs.

Sample paragraphs
Temporary exhibitions
At present, the museum only has one permanent exhibition but people might visit more often if there were different objects for them to see each time. Obviously this would require financial support. The museum could organise special exhibitions on a monthly basis if funding was available.
Evening events
The museum opening hours are very limited and unless it extends these, working adults won't come through its doors. On certain evenings, the museum could hold a series of talks. These would be more popular if visitors didn't have to pay for them on top of the entrance charge.

5 Ask students to work in pairs, deciding on a further problem and possible recommendations. Elicit their ideas.

Suggested answers

Problems	Recommendations
closes too early	*extend the opening times*
not much choice	*have a broader menu*
uncomfortable	*replace the furniture*
too expensive	*reduce the price*

6

Answers

Sentences a, c, d and f would have a positive effect.
Improvements to b and e:

b As the old furniture needs replacing, the college could opt for slightly more comfortable chairs.

e It is worth meeting students' needs, as the café will then be far more popular.

7 Set the report for homework.

Sample answer

REPORT ON THE EXISTING AND PROPOSED COLLEGE CAFE

Introduction

This report outlines the issues raised in relation to the college café and makes recommendations on how these problems could be addressed.

Opening times

At present, the opening hours are too limited. Apart from Saturdays, the café closes at 18.30, just when many students are leaving the library and likely to want to purchase a meal or drinks.

Menu

The lack of choice puts many students off using the café. Vegetarians feel that they are not being catered for and would like to see a range of healthy options.

Furniture

The tables and chairs in the present café are old and basic. There is nowhere to sit comfortably with friends, as you would find in the cafés in town.

Pricing policy

A common complaint is that most dishes are overpriced and are not affordable on a student budget. If possible, this needs to be reviewed.

Recommendations

From all of the above points, it is clear that several improvements could be made, from replacing the furniture to widening the choice of meals. If the opening hours could be extended and the prices reduced slightly, the new café would undoubtedly be more popular with students.

(202 words)

SB pages 46–47

Lesson plan	
Topic review	15–20 minutes
Grammar	10–15 minutes
Phrasal verbs	10–15 minutes
Tense revision	30–40 minutes

SV Omit the Topic review; allow students to do Phrasal verbs for homework, with an English–English dictionary.

LV Ask students to write short compositions, 60–80 words each, on two of the review topics.

The aim of this unit is to go over some of the main points covered in Units 1–6. With the exception of the Topic review, this unit can be done as a test or for homework.

Topic review

1 Ask students to work in pairs. They need to look at a–j and talk about whether the statements are true for them or not. Encourage them to go into detail, not just say 'yes' or 'no'. The point of this exercise is to get students to use some of the vocabulary and language they have studied, but in a personalised way. This part of the Revision unit is designed to be integrated with the other revision exercises if wanted, or to be done completely separately.

Teaching extra

Display the posters which students made of the vocabulary dealt with in Units 1–6 (see page 11). Students should spend some time revising this vocabulary and then the posters are taken down. Ask students to form groups, in order to play a form of the word game *Pictionary*. Write 15–20 words or phrasal verbs or expressions on separate slips of paper. Fold the slips over so no one can see what is written on them. The pieces of paper are put in the centre of the table and students take it in turns to pick up a slip and then draw something to represent whatever is written there, e.g. *to drown* can be drawn as a drowning man in the sea. The other students have to guess what the word or phrase is. You can make the game as easy or as difficult as you like depending on the words you choose to revise.

Grammar

2 This passage is about the sort of claims an insurance company receives from holidaymakers. The stories are all true. Students should read through the passage carefully and then fill in the gaps with ONE word only.

Answers
1 on 2 the 3 has 4 while/when
5 was 6 too 7 as/because 8 who

Phrasal verbs

3 This section is divided into three sections – phrasal verbs with *up*, with *out*, and then verbs/phrases that can be replaced with a phrasal verb. All the phrasal verbs tested here appear in Units 1–6. This exercise would make a good dictionary exercise – it is essential to get students used to using an English–English dictionary at an early stage. Translation dictionaries should be kept at home and used as a last resort.

If students are finding this exercise difficult, and most do, then give them some clues to help them. Tell them how many letters are in the word, maybe what the first letter is, etc. Encouragement should be the key here.

Answers
a save b gone c dress d keep e ring/call/phone
f stand g check h go i work j cut down
k stopped over l take back m set off
n to keep away from o take off

Revision of present and past tenses

4 Ask students to read through the passage carefully and then decide on the correct present or past tense for the verbs. Sometimes more than one answer is correct.

Answers
1 are   2 seems   3 are   4 sees
5 has tried / has been trying   6 has done / has been doing
7 has developed   8 is   9 puts / has put   10 has had
11 came   12 had never flown   13 had had
14 had taken / took   15 had never worried
16 announced   17 had   18 tried
19 overcame / had overcome
20 managed / had managed

5 This exercise has the type of question found in Paper 1 Part 4. Students should keep in mind that there is a maximum of five words only, and that contractions count as two words. In the exam there are only six questions in Part 4.

Answers
1 wouldn't go dancing unless
2 worst film I've ever
3 would have met you
4 aren't allowed to
5 more frightened of ghosts than
6 shouldn't have bought you
7 had (already) started
8 see to drive without

7 Life's too short

7.1

Vocabulary	Sports equipment
Speaking	Discussion using gerunds for likes and dislikes
Grammar focus	Gerunds and infinitives 1
Exam skills	Reading and Use of English Paper 1 Part 4

7.2

Speaking	Dangerous sports
Exam skills	Listening Paper 3 Part 3
	Reading and Use of English Paper 1 Part 3
	Speaking Paper 4 Part 3
Vocabulary	Collocations – sports
	Expressions with *do*

Workbook contents

Reading and Use of English Paper 1 Part 6 – gapped text
Grammar – gerunds and infinitives
Vocabulary – sport
Writing – Part 2 email

7.1 SB pages 48–49

Lesson plan
Speaking	15–30 minutes
Grammar	50–60 minutes

SV Set 7 or 8 for homework.
LV See Extension activity for 1.

Gerunds and infinitives 1

1 In pairs, students look at the illustrations of the different sports equipment a–o. They write down what each is called. If time allows, this exercise can be done as a quiz in teams.

Answers
a ice skates – ice skating   **b** swimming goggles and hat
c shuttlecock – badminton   **d** basket for basketball
e squash racket and ball   **f** rugby ball
g football   **h** table tennis bats and ball
i baseball bat   **j** oars – rowing   **k** tennis racket and ball
l volleyball   **m** snowboard – snowboarding
n golf clubs and ball   **o** ski poles and skis – skiing

Extension activity

Put students in teams and then ask one team to describe the rules of a game. The other team has to guess what the game is.

2 In pairs, students ask each other questions a–f. Draw students' attention to the fact that some of the questions contain an *-ing* word.

Teaching extra

Point out that many verbs and phrases to do with liking and disliking are followed by *-ing*:
can't stand hate dislike loathe detest don't mind
adore love be keen on feel like enjoy be interested in

3 Explain that a gerund is a verb in the *-ing* form which is used as a noun. It is important to point out that not all *-ing* forms are gerunds. The exercise is designed to make students aware of this.

Answers
a adjective (describing the kind of rope)
b participle (past continuous tense)
c gerund (gerund – subject of sentence)

4 Explain that students need to match sentences 1–5 with a–e. The aim is to make them aware of the common uses of the gerund in English.

Answers
a 2 **b** 4 **c** 5 **d** 1 **e** 3

5 Some verbs and adjectives are followed by a preposition and we usually use a gerund after them. Students should watch out for verbs followed by *to* as a preposition. Common ones are *look forward to doing* and *object to doing*. They are frequently tested. There is a selection of common verbs which are followed by a gerund in the Grammar folder, page 169.

Answers
a about getting   **b** of learning   **c** at teaching
d for dropping   **e** in doing   **f** at swimming
g to playing

6 This exercise looks at the infinitive. Explain that an infinitive is usually, but not always, *to* plus the base verb, e.g. *to do*. Students need to match sentences 1–6 with a–f (the different ways in which the infinitive is used). Before they start, check that they understand the terms in a–f.

Answers
a 3 **b** 5 **c** 2 **d** 1 **e** 4, 5 **f** 4, 6

Corpus spot

Ask the class to read through the sentences and talk about what is wrong with them in pairs.

Answers
a I should give up **swimming** every morning.
b Do you want **to** go out with me?
c I'm used to **sleeping** in a tent. / **I used to** sleep in a tent.
d There's no point **(in) playing** today.
e I suggest **(that)** you **go** to the sports centre. / I suggest **going** to the sports centre.
f I really enjoy **reading** about the old tennis stars.
g I recommend **(that)** you **go** there.
h I hope **to hear** from you soon.
i I am interested **in receiving** documentation about the courses.
j I agree **that you should find** a job.

---

7 Students read through the email before doing the exercise. They then have to decide whether to change the verb in brackets to a gerund or add *to* or leave the verb as it is.

Answers
1 climbing   2 tell   3 arriving   4 training
5 to assess   6 to make   7 to teach
8 mountaineering   9 to use   10 to work
11 climbing   12 to sleep   13 Reaching   14 jumping
15 seeing   16 tell

8 Gerunds and infinitives are frequently tested in Paper 1 Part 4. This exercise can be set for homework, if time is short.

Answers
1 accused Pete of pushing
2 is too wet to
3 had difficulty (in) learning
4 advised me not to go / advised me against (going)
5 would rather go on

7.2 SB pages 50–51

Lesson plan	
Speaking	5 minutes
Listening	15–20 minutes
Vocabulary	20–40 minutes
Speaking	15–20 minutes

SV   Set 7 and 8 or 9 for homework.
LV   See Extension activity for 4.

Speaking

1 The photos show three examples of extreme or dangerous sports: heli-skiing, free-style mountain biking and sky diving. Ask the class to discuss the questions in pairs.

Listening

2 **1 08** Refer students to the Exam spot. This part of the unit is looking at Paper 3 Part 3. The students hear five people speaking and have to match each speaker to one of eight options. Play the first extract and ask students to name the sport. They may not know the name in English, but will be familiar with what it is. (The recording script is given below.)

Answers
bungee jumping
Clues are: Dangerous Sports Club, ground seemed far away, jumps, attached to a rope

3 **1 09** Ask students to read through the options and check that they understand what they mean. Play the recording twice and ask students to mark down their answers.

Answers
1 F   2 A   3 D   4 C   5 G

Recording script
Speaker 1: All of us in the office where I work love doing it, <u>probably because we're all desperate to get out of that 9 to 5 routine</u>. It's an expensive sport but we all joined a Dangerous Sports Club to help keep costs down. The first time I did it I really was frightened as the ground seemed so far away, but I said to myself that nothing would happen and I wasn't going to die. I did my first two jumps in Canada and London. Apparently, in Germany they're doing it without being attached to a rope, but with just a net beneath. That could be pretty scary, couldn't it?

Speaker 2: About four years ago I was very ill and nearly died. Sometime later I was involved in a serious car crash. It made me realise how risky everyday life is, and it seemed to cure me of fear, so I said to myself, why not push things to the limit? So, I had a go at white-water rafting in the States and then moved on to other things. It's been brilliant. I've done all sorts of things, from abseiling down mountains to skydiving. <u>Now I try to keep giving myself difficult and exciting things to do</u> – not that I've got anything to prove, it's just a personal thing really. I'm thinking of doing river sledging next.

Speaker 3: I took part in a trek to ski across the Arctic last year. It was probably the most dangerous thing I've ever done, but I'd do it again tomorrow. <u>I was conscious all the time that death was very near and in a strange way that made it seem more fun.</u> I cried in absolute terror sometimes, especially when the ice began to melt and great holes would suddenly appear just in front of me. It was the ultimate challenge for a skier like myself and I guess I'm not afraid of anything any more. In fact, I'm looking forward to skiing in the Antarctic next year!

Speaker 4: I've always enjoyed diving as it's quite an exciting sport, but last winter I had the ultimate experience of going shark-feeding in the Caribbean. The sharks were about three metres in length and obviously they are quite aggressive and can bite you, but if you put on the right protective clothing and take precautions <u>it's no more of a risk than driving fast motor cars. I must say I had more accidents when I went horse riding.</u> I did feel a bit nervous as I went over the side of the boat – after all, I've seen stories about shark attacks on TV like everyone else! But I was never in any real danger.

Speaker 5: Some of my mates had started doing this free climbing – you know where you don't use ropes, only your hands and feet. I guess they needed to have a bit of excitement in their lives, didn't they? Me, I think I get enough from my job as a motorbike courier in London. Anyway, I went with them one weekend. It was terrifying and I was sure I'd end up lying in a hospital bed, but <u>I felt I had to do it, especially with them looking on.</u> There was no pressure from them, but you know how it is. Anyway, I did my best and I have to say it gave me a real 'buzz'. I can understand why people go in for this type of thing now.

4

Answers
1 bungee jumping
2 white-water rafting, abseiling, skydiving, river sledging (going down rapids on a small sledge)
3 skiing
4 diving, driving fast cars, horse riding
5 free climbing (without a rope or harness)

Extension activity

You heard these words in the listening extracts. In pairs, talk about what kind of words they are and then change them into nouns.

a dangerous   d protective
b frightened   e nervous
c risky   f terrifying

Answers
a danger   b fright/fear   c risk   d protection
e nerve, nerves   f terror

Vocabulary

5 **This exercise checks students know the names of places where sports take place.**

Answers
do aerobics – gym, studio
do martial arts – gym, studio
go swimming – (swimming) pool
do athletics – track, stadium
play basketball – court
do gymnastics – gym, studio
go snowboarding – piste
play golf – course
go running – track
play football – pitch, stadium

6 **Ask students to use an English–English dictionary to decide on the right word and also to check on the meaning and use of the other word.**

Answers
a laps   b spectators   c referee   d sets   e goal

7

Answers
a do business with   b do for a living
c are doing / did a good job   d did (a lot of) damage
e did me a favour   f do their best   g do without

8 Alternatively this exercise could be done in writing for homework.

9 This exercise can be set for homework, if time is short. Students read through the article and decide what changes need to be made to the word in brackets so that it makes sense in the sentence.

Background information

A personal trainer is a person who comes to your house to encourage you to work out or who works with you individually at the gym. Many film stars employ a trainer so that they can exercise in private.

Answers

1 ensure   **2** training   **3** uncertain   **4** demanding
5 Movement   **6** Education   **7** qualification(s)
8 freedom

Speaking

10 Refer the students to the Exam spot. Check that they are familiar with the useful language section. Ask the students to get into pairs or threes. They should make sure that they give their partner a chance to speak and that they come to a conclusion at the end of their discussion.

Exam folder 4

SB pages 50–51

Paper 1 Part 1
Multiple-choice cloze

Although this is the first part of Paper 1, students should realise that they can do the seven parts of the paper in any order they want. Make sure students read through the advice which is given in this part of the Exam folder, especially about reading the passage from beginning to end before they start deciding on answers. They might easily get an answer wrong if they don't understand the meaning of the whole passage. There are eight gaps and four options for each gap, with an example at the beginning.

In this introduction there are five categories of words which are often tested on this part of the paper. They are:

Expressions
Verb/Adjective + preposition
Phrasal verbs
Linking words
Vocabulary

Ask students to read through the categories and look at the examples. These explain how to get the correct answer.

Students should then read through the passage on the history of football very carefully. Although they are not allowed to have a dictionary in the examination, it is good policy for them to use an English–English dictionary in class and at home.

Put students in pairs and ask them to decide on the correct option: A, B, C or D. They should also be able to give a reason for their choice.

Answers

1 C   **2** A   **3** A   **4** B   **5** A   **6** C   **7** C   **8** D

Growing up

8.1

Exam skills	Speaking Paper 4 Parts 2 and 4
	Reading and Use of English Paper 1 Part 5

8.2

Grammar focus	*used to* and *would*
Vocabulary	Collocations
	Phrasal verbs with *get*
Exam skills	Reading and Use of English Paper 1 Part 3

Workbook contents

Listening Paper 3 Part 3 – multiple matching
Vocabulary – collocations, definitions
Grammar – *used to* and *would*

8.1 SB pages 54–55

Lesson plan

Speaking	15–20 minutes
Reading	40–50 minutes
Speaking	10–20 minutes
SV	Omit 5.
LV	See Extension activity for 5.

Speaking

1 Ask the students to look at the photos and answer the questions in pairs.

2 It is important that students compare the photos, not just describe them.

The photos show

1 children playing together outdoors

2 a child playing a computer game indoors

3 a girl lying in her room looking at her laptop and listening to her music player

4 a boy helping out at home

Reading

3 Refer students to the Exam spot on page 55. Ask them to skim the text and decide whether the writer had a happy or unhappy childhood. The answer is probably a happy one.

4 Ask students to look at question 1 and the explanation for the answer. Then get them to do the rest of the questions, making sure that they are aware of the different types of question that they might meet on this paper. There are always six questions and as well as detail questions there could be reference, idiom and global questions.

Remind students that there will often be a question on an item of vocabulary, such as a word which is unusual or idiomatic, or one that is used by the writer in a special way. They should work out the meaning by looking at the context around the word itself.

Answers

1 B 2 D 3 C 4 A 5 B 6 B

5 Finish the topic with a discussion based on these questions.

Extension activity

The following are all nouns. Ask the students to read through the text again and find the adjectives which are related to these nouns. The nouns are in the same order as the adjectives appear in the text.

identity terror criticism confidence adventure sense

8.2 SB pages 56–57

Lesson plan

Grammar	30–40 minutes
Vocabulary	20–30 minutes
Speaking	10–15 minutes
SV	Omit 4; set 5 for homework.
LV	See Extension activities for 3 and 4.

used to and *would*

1 The aim of this section is to clarify the differences between *would do* and *used to do* and also between *used to do* and *be/get used to doing*. Students often confuse these structures and it is important that they can differentiate them as they are often tested.

would / used to

Students usually know *used to* at this level but might not be familiar with *would* used in this way. If they find it a problem, give them some more examples:
When I lived in Paris I would take taxis everywhere, eat in restaurants and go out every night.

Point out that we can use *used to* when we use *would* but we can't always use *would* for *used to*:
We can say: *I used to have long hair.*
We can't say: *I would have long hair.*
We can say: *I used to go to town on the bus.*
We can also say: *I would go to town on the bus.*

This is because we don't use *would* for past states or situations – only for past actions. Students might ask why they have to learn it and the simple answer is that it is a very common structure in narratives and also that it is tested in the exam. *Would* is more formal than *used to*.

> **Answers**
> **a** 1   **b** 3   **c** 2
> *I'm used to living away from home.* – The speaker has probably lived away from home for some time and is used to it.
> *I'm getting used to living away from home.* – The speaker probably hasn't lived away from home for long and is **not** completely used to it yet.

2 Draw students' attention to the Corpus spot.

> **Answers**
> **a** used to have   **b** *correct*   **c** *correct*
> **d** get used to doing
> **e** used to work / was used to working
> **f** *correct*   **g** used to go

3 *be/get used to doing* and *used to do*

The problem that arises here is not usually in understanding the concept, more in getting the structure correct. Ask students in pairs to compare their past with their present. For example:
I used to get up at seven o'clock when I was at school. Now I have a job, I've had to get used to getting up earlier – at six thirty.

Point out that *be/get used to doing* can be used with all tenses.

Refer students to the Grammar folder, page 169.

Ask the students to discuss the questions in pairs or in groups.

> **E**xtension activity
>
> For more oral practice, put students in pairs and ask them to talk about their relationship with their grandparents when they were younger, only using *would*. For example:
> *My grandmother would let me help her do the baking.*
> *My grandfather would take me fishing.*
> Alternatively, students could talk about different periods in the past – the Stone Age, the Ancient Egyptians, etc. Divide the students into groups and ask them to choose a certain time period. Get them to write down five or six sentences about what children *used to do* / *would do* during that time, and then ask them to read them out to the class.

Vocabulary

4 Students should decide which is the correct collocation.

> **Answers**
> **a** do   **b** break   **c** having   **d** made   **e** kept
> **f** tastes   **g** spends

> **E**xtension activity
>
> Working with a partner, students ask and answer the following questions:
> • Are you good at keeping secrets?
> • Do you ever break promises?
> • What keeps you awake at nights?
> • Which food tastes really good / really strange?
> • Is there anything which you spend too much time doing?

5 Ask students to complete the sentences.

> **Answers**
> **a** the angry neighbour   **b** some work
> **c** washing the floor   **d** the flu   **e** the tennis team
> **f** not paying

6 Students ask and answer the questions in pairs.

7

> **Answers**
> **1** separation   **2** social   **3** happiness   **4** preference
> **5** ability   **6** unconsciously   **7** behaviour/behavior
> **8** remarkable

8 Ask the students to ask and answer the questions in pairs or groups.

Writing folder 4

SB pages 58–59

Paper 2 Part 1 Essays

Refer students to the information at the top of the page and look back at Writing folder 2 if necessary.

1   Give students time to read the exam question and look at the plan.

2   Ask students to match the plan to paragraphs A–E.

Answers
1 D   2 B   3 A   4 E   5 C

3   Elicit alternative adjectives.

Possible answers
substantial (earnings) – high
essential (job) – vital
real (issue) – actual
strong (feelings) – firm beliefs
central (place) – key

4   Check understanding of the linkers and elicit the three types.

Answers
Addition: as well as, furthermore
Contrast: at the same time, in contrast, nevertheless
Result: as a result, consequently

5   Refer students to the Assessment focus. Then ask them to read the exam question and add their ideas to the diagram.

6

Sample answer

FITNESS WHEN WORKING HARD

Physical exercise is generally believed to be good for the mind as well as the body. This essay considers its place in a busy lifestyle, looking at the advantages to health but also considering possible drawbacks.

People in stressful jobs with a heavy workload can profit enormously from taking regular exercise. Similarly, students who work late at night to meet essay deadlines will function better if they leave their desk for a run or play tennis for an hour.

Aside from the obvious improvements to health and fitness, such as being in better shape and keeping weight under control, people who take exercise sleep more soundly. This is because they are physically exhausted.

At the same time, there are some drawbacks in committing to regular exercise, not least the expense. Joining a gym usually requires a monthly fee. As well as the cost, taking time out of a busy schedule is not always easy. Nevertheless, the benefits outweigh the disadvantages.

In conclusion, setting aside time each day for exercise brings rewards. For those who spend most of their waking hours at a computer, whether working or studying, physical activity seems especially important.

(192 words)

9 The hard sell

9.1
Grammar focus	Modals 2: Speculation and deduction
Exam skills	Reading and Use of English Paper 1 Part 2
Vocabulary	Adjective–noun collocations

9.2
Exam skills	Listening: identifying opinions Listening Paper 3 Part 4
Vocabulary	Expressions for discussing ideas
Grammar extra	Order of adjectives

Workbook contents

Reading and Use of English Paper 1 Part 6 – gapped text
Grammar – modals of speculation and deduction
Reading and Use of English Paper 1 Part 4 – key word transformations
Vocabulary – advertising; collocations

9.1 SB pages 60–61

Lesson plan
Grammar	50–65 minutes
Vocabulary	5–10 minutes
Speaking	10–15 minutes
SV	Set 6 as homework.
LV	See Extension activity for 4.

Modals 2

1 Allow students around three minutes to speculate about the advert in pairs. Encourage them to use the sentence openers given, which exemplify the target structures for this lesson. Students can then look at the complete advert and slogan on page 85. The advert is for a Samsung 3D LED TV.

2 Ask students to read the information given in pairs and then discuss the second pair of examples.

Answer
No, in these examples, the speaker is certain (*must be*; *can't be*).

Now ask students to look at the final example given and to try saying the statement to each other with and without the question mark.

Answer
When the sentence is read as a statement, the speaker is certain (the use of *possibly* reinforces this certainty). However, when a question mark is added, the utterance becomes a speculation (and the use of *possibly* becomes a 'hedging' device). As a question, it would sound better with the words *could it* at the end.

Refer students to the Grammar folder, page 170, and ask them to read the first four points. Note the use of the question tag in the first example of the fourth point.

3 First, ask students to skim the text to find out what type of product the advert described in the article is for.

Answer
a hand cream

Now ask students to read the text again more carefully, underlining all the examples of modal verbs. Don't draw attention to the example of a past action (*must have won*), as this is the focus of 5.

Answers
3rd paragraph: can't be; Might it be; Could it be
4th paragraph: must have won; couldn't win

4 Ask students to work through a–f in pairs.

Answers
a spoken commentary played over a film
b a short, memorable tune, often with words, used to advertise a product
c someone famous
d decision
e a type of product made by a particular company
f clever

Check understanding of *brand non-attributes*, pointing out that the text goes on to explain this in the rest of the third paragraph. Remind students not to panic if they don't understand every word when they are reading; as this text shows, they will probably be able to deduce the meaning from the surrounding information.

Ask students to explain why the title is appropriate.

Extension activity

Ask students whether they can suggest another exploitation of 'brand non-attributes', for example showing people who *wouldn't* use the product to reinforce the target users. Ask them to discuss in pairs why this approach might be effective in selling a product.

5 Remind students of the example of a past action in the text and then ask them to discuss examples a–c in pairs.

Answers
a sure   b sure   c unsure

Refer students to the explanation and examples in the Grammar folder, page 170.

6 If this is being done in class, suggest students work through the Paper 1 Part 2 text on their own and then compare their answers in pairs.

Answers
1 every/each   2 than   3 of   4 up
5 making/being   6 himself   7 against   8 would

Vocabulary

7 Ask students to work in pairs, listing the possible phrases. Allow them five minutes for this.

Answers

huge:	variety, budget, market, picture
high:	budget, voice
low:	budget, voice
deep:	message, character, voice
shallow:	message, idea, character
narrow:	picture, view (also narrow ideas)
wide:	variety, market, picture

8 Put students into groups of three. Those on the left side of the room follow instructions for Group A, while the others follow Group B's instructions, which are on page 85.

Allow students adequate time to prepare for the role play (at least five minutes). Recommend that they decide on their individual roles within the group, as well as discussing who will say what.

Move round the room to check on progress and supply any vocabulary needed. Try to make sure that dictionaries are available.

Match each Group A with a Group B, and ask the Group B students to move in order to join their Group A. Tell students that they will have five minutes for the face-to-face discussion, asking them to try to reach an agreement within this time. Then elicit the outcome of each meeting to find out what was agreed.

Teaching extra

Role play can be an effective way of getting students to express themselves more fluently, particularly when opposing ideas are involved, as these often provoke extreme reactions! Encourage students to use their imagination to the full, giving them some initial suggestions if necessary.

9.2 SB pages 62–63

Lesson plan	
Listening	40–50 minutes
Grammar extra	0–10 minutes
Vocabulary	10 minutes
Speaking	20 minutes
SV	Set Grammar extra for homework.
LV	See Extension activity after 3.

Listening

1 Use the board to summarise vocabulary that comes up during this discussion. Start by reminding students of relevant vocabulary from 9.1: *special effects, voice-over, jingle, brand,* etc. Elicit other words and expressions that are useful for structuring the discussion.

Students discuss their favourite / least favourite commercials in pairs for about three minutes. Remind them that they should explain why they like or don't like them.

2 🔊 **1 10** Allow students a minute to look through phrases a–h. Then play the recording, asking them to tick the phrases as they listen. Explain that this is to help them to listen out for key information.

Answers
a, d, f and h are mentioned.

Recording script
Part 1

Man: There's one car advert that opens with part of a song by Bjork – it must have <u>cost a *fortune* to make</u>, and it looks tremendous …

Woman: I've seen that one. You're not sure what it's advertising to begin with, are you? A graceful silver vehicle <u>moving through an unusual landscape</u> … it could be a spacecraft of the future. All very stylish. The trouble is, it's a bit of a let-down when you realise it's just another *car* advert!

Man: Yes, <u>the beginning *is* a bit misleading</u> … It's funny, isn't it, sometimes the most effective ads are the really simple ones – you know, like a football manager sitting down at the breakfast table with his family, enjoying a particular cereal …

Woman: … he eats it, so it *must* be good. And <u>that actress from *Friends*</u> advertising shampoo – Jennifer Aniston, wasn't it? You know, seeing famous people on screen can be a huge influence on us. We see them as … well, as role models.

Man: Definitely. The ads they put on TV before the World Cup or the Olympics always use mega stars, don't they?

Woman: Yeah, remember the one that had a *whole team* of top footballers from around the world! The special effects were incredible – <u>the budget must have been *huge* … all for *one* advert!</u>

Man: But the company probably earned *millions* of dollars in increased sales, so for them it was worth it.

Check understanding and explain that students will hear the recording again later in the lesson.

3 🔊 **11 Explain that students will hear the same speakers talking about one specific advertisement, which is for Bacardi rum. Ask students to read through statements 1–4 before they listen.**

Answers
1 M   **2** W   **3** M   **4** W

Recording script
Part 2

Woman: There's one advert I really like, partly because it's brilliantly put together …

Man: And it's for …?

Woman: Bacardi – it's set on a tropical island somewhere in the Caribbean. And there's this radio DJ who's broadcasting in a studio and …

Man: Oh no, not Ray on Reef Radio?

Woman: You've seen it too!

Man: Yep. <u>Detest it, actually</u>. All about some friend of Ray's who's leaving for the mainland and how he's going to miss his wonderful life on the island …

Woman: And you see what he's been up to – I adore the way the DJ, Ray, tells the storyline on air and you see flashbacks of the other guy like 'I know you're going to miss the way they serve Bacardi around here' – and you see a girl throw a glassful in the friend's face! Such a striking image and <u>totally unexpected</u>.

Man: Mmm, I suppose ads do work well when they contain something out of the ordinary – I guess they stick in your mind that way.

Woman: Right … and of course, the ending itself is unforgettable – quite spectacular, isn't it? Seeing the friend sailing away on the boat, listening to all this on his radio – and then, what does he do … ?

Man: He dives off the deck and swims back to the island.

Woman: For another night on the town and a glass of …

Man: Yes, yes … You know, I must admit that although I personally loathe the ad, it sells the product pretty well. It's got the right ingredients – you know, exotic location, powerful images …

Woman: So what *didn't* you like about it?

Man: The characters themselves, I think … especially Ray!

Woman: Oh, but come on, <u>the very fact that you remember him now means he made an impact on you … which must mean that the ad has worked.</u>

Man: <u>True enough</u> … And what about you? You said it makes you laugh. Is that why you like it so much?

Woman: That … and the way it succeeds in telling a story in such a short time. I think that's quite clever, getting the message across like that. <u>The music's great, too.</u>

Man: But was it *truly* successful? I mean, did you dig into your pocket and buy a bottle?

Woman: Well, no … I don't drink spirits! I bet plenty of people were persuaded to rush out and buy some, though …

Check understanding of the following phrases, used in the Part 2 recording:

stick in your **mind** – stay in your memory, i.e. not be forgotten
make *an impact on* – have an effect on someone or something
get *the message across* – make someone understand something

Ask students to use an English–English dictionary to find other phrases to do with understanding and decision-making featuring the words in bold above. For example:

mind – change your mind, make up your mind / make your mind up, bear/keep something in mind, cross your mind
make – make sense, make the most of something, make the best of something, make up your mind
get – get your point/ideas across, get the feeling/idea/impression

4   Refer students to the Exam spot and explain that Part 4 is a multiple-choice listening task with three options. Students will need to listen carefully, as all three options will be referred to in the recording in some way.

Ask students to read the question and options, underlining key words. Elicit these and draw students' attention to the verb 'agree' in the question itself: they must find an opinion that is shared by both speakers. Play the extract and elicit the correct answer (C).

Ask students to vote for the best commercial currently showing on television or at the cinema. Select a shortlist of four commercials and ask students to award each of them points (1 = good, 2 = very good, 3 = excellent) for any of the following categories that apply. They can do this in groups or as a whole class.

Storyline   Images   Actors   Voice-over   Music   Slogan   Message

Add up the points and announce the winning commercial.

5   ▶ **12** Before playing the recording, ask students to read questions 1–4 and underline the key words. Stop the recording between each question and review answers, referring to the recording script if necessary.

Answers
1 B   2 B   3 C   4 A

Recording script

Interviewer: In the studio with me today is Don Cooper, who has been very successful in producing commercials for television. Don, what is the most important thing to get right in this type of advertising?

Don: Well, I've made at least thirty commercials for television over the last few years, so I reckon I know pretty much what the magic ingredients are. I used to think that the setting was all-important, but I've come to realise that you can have the most exotic location in the world and a truly fantastic storyline, but your commercial will not succeed if you ignore the people factor. It takes time and effort to select the perfect individuals to play your characters but by getting this right, you'll draw your target audience in, make them relate to what's on the screen, and hopefully persuade them that they want a piece of what they're seeing. It's as simple as that.

Interviewer: Mmm, I see. And what advice would you give to anyone writing a script? What's crucial there?

Don: The average TV commercial runs for just 30 seconds so you haven't got long to get your message across. Don't opt for long, flowery sentences – keep it short and punchy. Not only that, but remember that some people might not actually be watching the screen while the commercial is on. My golden rule is to mention the product itself in the audio, so that anyone who has wandered off to make coffee or check the kids' homework will still pick up on it.

Interviewer: Right! Now, your work is very creative, but is it difficult to keep coming up with new ways of promoting the same product?

Don: That can become a challenge, yes. If a company likes what you're doing, as likely as not you'll be asked to make more than one commercial for a product over time, so it seems to me that consistency is an important issue. If you use the same voice-over, or a jingle that echoes the last one in some way, you start to strengthen the company's image, and if the viewer begins to recognise the brand through links like these, you're halfway there already. The drawback with all of this is that you may have to walk away from new business, in order to concentrate on a small number of favourite clients.

Interviewer: And when you're ready to broadcast a commercial, how do you decide on where to show it – and when?

Don: Selecting the most appropriate time and place for your finished commercial is absolutely crucial. Having it go out at three in the morning will save you money, but in actual fact, there's little point in doing this if your core audience, however large or small, is fast asleep! The same holds true for where you choose to broadcast your ad: a bad match between product and station can only spell disaster, so avoid it at all costs.

Interviewer: Well many thanks Don, we'll be back to you with listeners' questions a bit later in the programme. In the meantime …

Grammar extra

Ask students to identify the opinion adjective and discuss the order of adjectives in the example.

Answer
The order cannot be changed because an opinion adjective (*graceful*) always comes first.

Ask students to work through the slogans in pairs, identifying the types of adjective used.

Answers
Opinion adjectives: classic, sensational, popular, delicious
Size: full-length, bite-sized
Age: new
Colour: navy
Nationality: British
Material: cotton, creamy

Students can do this exercise either in pairs in class, or for homework. Refer them to the Grammar folder, page 170, for further explanation.

Answers
a a huge black dog
b *correct*
c the famous Italian singer
d a large red apple
e an elaborate square wooden box
f a sophisticated new novel by a tremendous Scottish author

Vocabulary

6   Remind students not to use *reckon* in any written exam answers apart from an informal letter. Elicit the other informal verbs (*bet, guess*) and give students a spoken example of each one.
I bet he's going to be late again!
I guess everyone has an ad that they can't stand.

7   Ask students to put the phrases into columns and elicit answers. Explain that these phrases will be useful in the shared task of the Speaking test (Paper 4 Part 3). It would also be perfectly acceptable to use the informal verbs in 6 (*I bet, I guess, I reckon*) to introduce their ideas and opinions in this part.

Answers
Introducing an opinion: I suppose …   It seems to me that …
Giving a different point of view: On the other hand, …
True enough, though …
Adding to an idea: Not only that, but …   What's more, …

Speaking

8   Allow students five minutes to prepare their ideas and list useful vocabulary. They should do this on their own and then compare notes with another student.

Here is some information about each billboard, which contains relevant vocabulary.

1   ***British Gas***
This is a leading gas supplier in Britain, which also sells and services appliances like cookers and central heating boilers. The ad is emphasising the scale of the company's household support, with its 7000 engineers ready to come out in their vans in the middle of the night to attend to an emergency. The slogan 'Looking after your world' is short and effective, and the image of the vans against the night sky is interesting.

2   ***Swiftcover car insurance***
This billboard features the well-known rock star Iggy Pop, who is being used to sell instant car insurance here (he also appears in TV commercials promoting the same company). The claim is that you can get a quote in 60 seconds and the number 60 is very prominently displayed. The stopwatch covering Iggy's right eye is quite a clever way of reinforcing the idea of limited time and the use of colour is quite strong.

3   ***Vodafone***
This billboard uses balls of knitting wool to represent a family and includes a play on the idiomatic phrase 'Be closer-knit'. The colours are very bright and contrast with the shade of red associated with the company. The two 'children' are formed from two different colours of wool, which is quite a striking image. They must be grown-up and living away from home though, or they wouldn't need to call their 'parents' on the phone.

4   ***Vauxhall cars***
Although this is one car advert among many, it uses the powerful image of a beach under different weather conditions. The idiomatic expression 'Come rain, come shine' implies that whatever the weather is like, this Vauxhall car will be perfect for you.

Tell students that they have three minutes to do the whole task. Remind them to use some of the phrases from 6 and 7 as well as phrases from Unit 7.

Elicit which adverts are seen as the most effective and why.

Exam folder 5

SB pages 64–65

Paper 3 Part 2
Sentence completion

1 Explain to students that they should use the 45 seconds before the recording starts to predict what they might hear. The key words and phrases are underlined for them here. This is primarily an awareness-raising activity, showing students how paraphrase and exemplification may operate in a Paper 3 context. It also highlights the benefits of working with recording scripts, at least in the early stages of a course. Give students time to read the four sentences and corresponding parts of the script.

2 🔊 13 Remind students that they should never write more than three words in a gap. Here, they need to write only one or two words. Tell students that the words must fit grammatically, including plurals if necessary. Play the recording and elicit answers.

Answers
1 washing powder   2 lifestyle   3 unusual behaviour
4 puppies (and) kittens

3 The actual answer sheet starts at question 9 as this is the first question in Part 2. Before students transfer their answers, check their spelling and remind them of the plural change to some nouns ending in -y, as in the example in 4: *puppies*. Remind them to use capital letters on the answer sheet.

4 Ask students to read the advice carefully.

5 🔊 14 The recording includes a 45-second pause.

Answers
1 company name	6 pop songs
2 (breakfast) cereal	7 lifestyle
3 direct promotion	8 downloading
4 dessert	9 (strong) emotional
5 (famous/well-known)	connection
songwriters	10 30/thirty seconds

Recording script
You will hear part of a talk about advertising jingles. For questions 1–10, complete the sentences with a word or short phrase. You now have 45 seconds to look at Part Two.

Today I'm going to consider the history of the commercial jingle. So, first of all, what is it? Well, it's a type of slogan that is set to music. It could be very simple, for example just a company name, if that's the most important message to get across.

Jingles have been in existence since the birth of commercial radio in the USA in the 1920s. It is generally believed that the modern commercial jingle took off on Christmas Eve 1926, when a group of four singers was heard performing a jingle for a breakfast cereal. The product in question had not been selling well but sales increased noticeably after the broadcast.

In the early 1930s, listening to the radio was very popular in the States – there was no television then of course. The rules on advertising did not permit the direct promotion of products during peak listening hours. The jingle was a clever way round this problem, and so advertisers started using them a lot. For example, one long-running radio series called *The Adventures of the Jenkins Family* began with a short rhyming jingle for a dessert. Interestingly, this product was the first of its type to be marketed in the United States, and the catchy rhyme made a big impact on the public.

In the 1950s, jingles became more sophisticated and famous songwriters were often signed up to write them. But by the 1980s, the public had grown tired of listening to jingles like these. Advertisers had to look for something else and they turned to pop songs. In 1987, the Beatles' tune *Revolution* was chosen for a Nike shoe campaign and this marked a revolution in advertising too. Showing a good product was simply not enough any longer – to be successful, a commercial now had to represent a whole lifestyle, which is essentially where we are today. Drawing on the shared cultural experience of music has become the most effective way to sell a product and, with the record industry losing money because of downloading, advertising companies have been very welcome business partners.

Psychologists who study the effects of music on the brain have found that music with a strong emotional connection to the listener is more memorable, and this has become an important area of research at one American university. Apparently, some songs contain a feature called an 'ear worm' – the term comes from a German word. An ear worm is a tiny piece of music of between 15 and 30 seconds that gets stuck in your head and tends to repeat itself. Popular examples include Queen's anthem *We will rock you* and the *Mission Impossible* theme tune. The world of advertising is excited by the possibilities here, so we can expect our heads to be full of ear worms before too long!

10 The final frontier

10.1

Exam skills	Speaking Paper 4 Part 2
	Reading and Use of English Paper 1 Part 6
Vocabulary	Word formation

10.2

Grammar focus	Review of future tenses
Listening	Global meaning
Vocabulary	Phrases with *at*

Workbook contents

Reading and Use of English Paper 1 Part 1 – multiple-choice cloze
Listening Paper 3 Part 4 – multiple choice
Grammar – future tenses
Writing – the future

10.1 SB pages 66–67

Lesson plan

Speaking	5–10 minutes
Reading	30 minutes
Vocabulary	20 minutes
Speaking	10–30 minutes

SV Elicit quick ideas in 1; keep discussion in 7 brief.
LV Extend the discussion in 7; see Extension activity for 7.

Speaking

1 The photos show (top) a still from the film *Mission to Mars* and (bottom) a conceptual computer artwork of 'spaceboarders' outside a space hotel orbiting Earth with the moon in the background. The hotel is constructed from used shuttle fuel tanks.

Teaching extra

If you have time, research a topic area further on the internet. For example, the Space Frontier Foundation has its own website (go to http://spacefrontier.org), and if you use a search engine, you will probably find many other relevant sites. Encourage students to do this for themselves as they will be using their English in a very practical way.

Reading

2 Suggest that students start by reading the title and opening paragraph, as this part of a newspaper or magazine article often holds many clues to the overall subject matter. Explain that in Paper 1 Part 6, the first paragraph does not contain a gap, but should be read carefully for content clues. Ask students to skim the rest of the article to answer the question.

Answers
NASA is government-owned whereas the SFF is encouraging private enterprise. NASA is seen as elitist, while the SFF wants to open up mass space travel. NASA doesn't share the SFF's belief in space tourism.

3 Refer students to the Exam spot. Ask students to check in pairs whether sentence A fits any of the gaps, using the underlined parts to help them. (Sentence A is the extra sentence.) Suggest students work on B–G in pairs.

Answers
1 D   2 G   3 B   4 F   5 C   6 E

Vocabulary

4 Remind students that the related words could have prefixes and/or suffixes.

Answers
b settlement   c commercial   d achievement
e endlessly   f inappropriate   g willingness
h affordable   i scientific   j impressive

5 Explain that negative prefixes such as these are tested in Paper 1. Refer students to Exam folder 2 on page 26 before they work through a–f.

Answers
a illegal   b inexperienced   c irresponsible
d immoral   e irregular   f impatient

6 Ask students to complete a–d in pairs and check their answers.

Answers
a impatient   b inexperienced   c illegal
d irregular

Speaking

7 These points could be handled as class discussion or in groups. Remind students to use some of the new vocabulary, especially the words from 4.

> ### Extension activity
>
> Set up a competition to decide which six students will go on the first spaceship to Mars. Every student takes on the role of a 'vital' individual and gives a brief explanation as to why they should go on the spaceship. For example:
> biosphere ecologist – to grow edible food crops on Mars
> comedian – to keep everyone entertained in the absence of television
> Encourage students to use their imagination and have a class vote to decide on the best ideas.

10.2 SB pages 68–69

Lesson plan	
Grammar	30–40 minutes
Listening	10–20 minutes
Vocabulary	20–30 minutes

SV	Set 6 for homework; omit discussion in 7.
LV	See Extension activity for 8.

Review of future tenses

1 Explain that this lesson reviews several ways of referring to the future, all of which students should already know. Suggest they work in pairs.

> **Answers**
> a future simple b *going to* future c future continuous
> d future perfect e *going to* future
> f present simple – *plans to* g present simple – *is due to*

2 Now ask students to match the four categories to examples a–g.

> **Answers**
> 1 (prediction) **a, b, c**
> 2 (planned event) **f, g**
> 3 (event that has not yet happened but is expected to happen within a period of time) **d**
> 4 (intention) **e**

3 Both examples use modals (*may, could*) to predict possible future events. Elicit the other modal that is used in this way (*might*). Ask students to compare the use of *will* for prediction: in sentence b – if it said *will* instead of *could*, what would the effect be? (*To make it more certain – will adds certainty to a prediction.*)

4 The sentence contains reported speech with backshift. David Ashford's words were probably 'Space tourism will begin ten years after people stop laughing at the concept.' This is then reported as '… once said space tourism would begin …'. Explain that students will be reviewing reported speech in Unit 13.

5 The photo shows the International Space Station. Allow students up to five minutes to complete the exercise and then check answers, eliciting reasons.

> **Answers**
> a will fall (not a continuous state)
> b won't be (prediction rather than definite truth)
> c may (prediction of possible future event)
> d will carry (future event + verb not tied to an end date)
> e am going to (definite plan for the near future; intention)
> f would (reported speech)
> g will be living (prediction, future truth)
> h will have been (anniversary has not yet happened)

6 Elicit students' reactions to the ideas given about clothing in the future. Ask students to complete the summary, explaining that one verb requires a passive form.

> **Answers**
> 1 will have risen   2 will have included
> 3 will have been filled   4 will have become
> 5 will have taken

Listening

7 **1 15** Students should listen for gist and global meaning in order to decide whether the speakers express positive or negative views. Play the recording a second time so that students can confirm their answers.

> **Answer**
> Speakers 1 and 2 express negative views; Speaker 3 is positive.

Recording script

Speaker 1: I find it quite scary actually. Films like *Bladerunner* could really come true. Imagine a city like Los Angeles in twenty years' time. I mean, it's dangerous now, isn't it – remember the riots? People will be living in run-down buildings, too frightened to come out. Oil supplies will have run out, so there won't be any cars. And with global warming and El Niño, the climate is changing, so the lack of sunlight and pouring rain in the film may well be accurate ... what LA weather will be like.

Speaker 2: I'm reading one of his sci-fi ones at the moment. It all happens way off in the future, thousands of years from now. There are human-like characters, but they're a very sophisticated race – we'll never be as clever as them! They live for at least three hundred years and after that they can choose to live on in a different state. And there's no poverty, no war ... For the human race, this seems impossible – there will always be some country at war with another. I don't see a long-term future for the human race ... even if our planet survives in one piece, we'll have wiped each other out or something.

Speaker 3: Things may be different, but they won't necessarily be any worse. We'll just enter a new phase of our culture, our existence. We've always adapted ... I mean, think of the huge changes with the Industrial Revolution ... why should this be any different? And as for the eco-threat, we're going to have to deal with it somehow, aren't we? I think we will. I can't accept that the human race will cease to be. Call me an optimist, but that's what I feel ...

Vocabulary

8   Explain to students that the preposition *at*, like *in* and *on*, commonly occurs in fixed phrases (sentences 1–3) and patterns (sentence 4). Ask students to complete the exercise and then list all the options, with their meanings or an example sentence, in their vocabulary notebooks.

Answers
1 B   **2** C   **3** A   **4** B

Extension activity

Write some adjectives on the board and ask students to come up with more examples of the pronoun and superlative pattern. For example:

silly: The children were at their silliest towards the end of the party.

mean: The cheap present showed my uncle at his meanest!

strong: With three players back from injury, Norwich City will be at their strongest tomorrow.

high: The dollar was at its highest for several months.

interesting: Live coverage is news at its most interesting.

Writing folder 5

Paper 2 Part 2 Articles

1 Elicit why people read articles in magazines and newspapers: usually for pleasure or for information. Explain to students that it is important for an article to engage or entertain the reader, and that a suitable title will help to do this. Ask students to decide in pairs which title most appeals to them.

2 Ask students to match the titles to the paragraphs. Point out that the opening paragraph for **B** does not pick up on the idea of a lifelong ambition. The other three titles are intriguing and the reader would probably want to continue reading.

Answers
A 3-2-1 Lift off!   **B** A lifelong ambition
C Aliens are coming ...   **D** Is anybody there?

3 Encourage students to use a variety of vocabulary in their writing. This exercise raises awareness of this and shows them the importance of improving a first draft.

Sample answer
(D, first stage)
On some nights, I open my window and gaze at the stars. It's a wonderful thing to do. Sometimes I stay there for ages, wondering what the universe holds. It makes me feel humble. Space is a vast place. There are so many galaxies apart from our own – so there must be other life?

Answers
a adjectives   **b** noun phrase   **c** quantifiers
d adverbs
Sample answer
(D, second stage)
On some beautiful, cloudless nights, I open my window and gaze at the twinkling stars. It's such a wonderful thing to do, so I sometimes stay there for ages, wondering what the universe holds. It makes me feel very humble as space is a truly vast place. There are so many galaxies apart from our own – so there must surely be other forms of life?

The photograph shows distant galaxies observed by the Hubble Space Telescope.

4

Sample answer
It has always been my dream to step on board a shiny, silver rocket and be launched into space. An article which I read recently said space travel may be possible for ordinary people soon. Wouldn't it be wonderful to be one of the first to go? I really hope that I am lucky enough to experience this.

5 Refer students to the Assessment focus and stress the importance of writing in a suitable style for an article. Then ask them to read through the exam task carefully. As they read, they should think about the magazine the article will appear in and its likely readers.

6 Students can discuss a–d in pairs.

Answers
a Future forms of transport; future destinations for holidays.
b More than one kind of transport should be mentioned.
c Given the type of magazine, it should be fairly lively and 'easy to read'.
d Probably four: an opening paragraph; one on transport; one on holidays; a final paragraph.

7 Tell students to use their imagination to the full when thinking of ideas. When they have finished their plan, suggest that they write a first draft, and then try to make improvements to it. Make sure that students understand that they will not have time to do a rough draft in the actual exam, but it is good practice for them at this stage of their preparation.

Sample answer
TRAVEL TO THE STARS
You are probably reading this on board a jumbo jet, but imagine how you could be travelling and where you might be able to get to on holiday in fifty years' time!

By then, planes could be seen as old-fashioned, with re-usable space rockets being used for holiday destinations instead. Or perhaps someone will have invented a completely new form of transport, capable of travelling faster than the speed of light?

If that ever happens, we will be able to go wherever we want to on holiday – not just within our own solar system, but out to other parts of our galaxy, or even to another galaxy further away. A cheap weekend break might consist of a couple of nights on an orbiting space station, watching the world below.

Just sit back in your seat, close your eyes, and dream of your future. Isn't it exciting!

11 Like mother, like daughter

11.1

Exam skills	Speaking Paper 4 Part 1
	Listening Paper 3 Part 4
Grammar extra	*like*
Speaking	Family resemblances and characteristics

11.2

Vocabulary	Adjectives describing personality
	Phrasal verbs and expressions with *take*
	Collocations – adverb or adjective?
Grammar focus	Past and present participles

Workbook contents

Reading and Use of English Paper 1 Part 3 – word formation

Vocabulary – word formation, word groups, American English

Writing – error correction, informal letter

11.1 SB pages 72–73

Lesson plan

Speaking	10–20 minutes
Listening	30–40 minutes
Speaking	20–30 minutes

SV   Omit 5 and 6.
LV   See Extension activity for 2.

Speaking

1   The photos show Tom Hanks and his son Colin, Madonna and her daughter Lourdes, and Will Smith and his son Jaden.

Ask students to look at the photos. They should think about the similarities and differences in the photos. The aim of this is to get students thinking and talking about themselves and their families.

Refer students to the Exam spot. At the beginning of the Speaking part of the examination, the examiner will chat to the two or three candidates about everyday things. They'll ask for personal information, about the candidates' studies or job, about their hobbies and future plans.

2   Students should talk to each other in pairs about themselves and their families. They need to answer questions on facial and body features, personality and sound. If they know each other very well, then you should ask them to find out three things about each other or their families that they didn't know before.

Extension activity

If you have time, then you can play the game of 20 questions. Think of a famous person but keep it to yourself. Then students have to ask questions to find out their identity. It must be someone they would have heard of, but don't make it too easy. When they get the idea, put them in pairs to practise.

Listening

3   🔊 16 Refer students to the Exam spot, then ask them to read through the questions and check if there is anything they don't understand. Play the recording twice.

Answers
1 B   2 B   3 C   4 B   5 A   6 C   7 B

Recording script

Presenter: So, Hannah, what was it like growing up in Hollywood as an only child, and having such a famous mother?

Hannah: Well, I guess I was pretty privileged as I had things most other kids only dream about. For instance, when I was 14 I just loved Harrison Ford films, and my mother arranged for me and a few friends to go to the film set to see him working on his latest film, as a treat for my birthday. I don't think I was particularly spoilt though, even though I was an only child, and I didn't get into trouble like some of the kids I knew did.

Presenter: You, yourself, are an actress now. Did she ever try to put you off acting?

Hannah: Not at all. Just the opposite. She felt I should follow my feelings, I guess in the same way she had done when she was younger. My grandparents hadn't wanted her to take up acting, you know, especially as she had to move from Europe to Hollywood. I don't think her family took her seriously at first and I think she was quite homesick and felt she could have done with a little more family support.

Presenter: Now, you look very like your mother, don't you?

Hannah: Oh, yes. My mouth, the shape of my face, my jaw line is my mother's. My nose too, but only the tip of it, not the bridge – that is unique, like no one else's in the family. My eyes, my forehead, my colouring, my height are different from my mother's but everyone tells me I look like her. When I say everybody, I mean everybody. People stop me in shops, on the subway, in the street.

Presenter: What does your mother say about this?

Hannah: Well, we both looked in the mirror one day and came to the same conclusion – people exaggerate. Then one day I went into a dress shop. I was alone except for another customer. I thought to myself, 'She looks like my mother.' Then I walked too close to her and crashed into a mirror – the lady was me! I hadn't recognised myself!

Presenter: What qualities do you think your mother possesses?

Hannah: Great physical energy. She used to walk fast, and when she wasn't acting she cleaned and organised the house perfectly. She loved acting more than cleaning; she loved acting most and above all. It took me some time not to feel hurt by this. I wanted to come first. When asked what was the most important thing in her life, she got real embarrassed and nervous, but my mother couldn't lie; she had to say 'acting'; though I know for our sake she wished she could say 'family'. She is terribly practical, and I am too. We consider it one of the greatest qualities in people. We give it the same status as intelligence. Practicality is what made my mother advise me to learn to be an accountant. 'If you know how to do it, you know you'll never be cheated out of any money,' she says. I didn't finish the course as I decided I wanted to act.

Presenter: Did she have any personal experience of being cheated out of money?

Hannah: Well, my mother has always been a very generous person to people she likes. I think another actor who she fell out with started the rumour that she is a bit stingy. She does say that I'm a bit extravagant.

Presenter: Now, you don't sound like your mother, do you?

Hannah: Oh no. She still has a bit of an accent. But her voice is definitely an actress's voice – the clearest speech, the most commanding delivery, and loud. The family used to tell her that she didn't need a phone, she could have just talked to us on the other side of town and we would have heard her. She justifies it with 'I picked it up in the theatre. My voice has to reach all the way to the last row.'

Presenter: Thank you for coming in today to talk to us, Hannah, and good luck in your new film, which I believe is released on Tuesday?

Hannah: Yes, that's right. Thank you.

4 Ask the students to read through the questions and then play the recording again.

Answers
a privileged   b homesick   c unique
d embarrassed and nervous   e being practical
f generous; stingy   g clear; commanding; loud

Grammar extra

This is just a short awareness exercise. Students often confuse these two uses of *like*:
What's she like?
What does she like?

Answers
A tall, friendly, amusing
B swimming, hamburgers, watching TV, photography

Speaking

5 This exercise is to get the class talking but possibly in a way that they haven't thought about before. It means they have to move round the room and form new groups, depending on what brothers and sisters they have. If there is a student who has no one in their group, ask him/her to go to each group in turn to talk about his/her experience. Care should be taken if you know there are people in the class who have family problems.

6 The aim of this exercise is to help practise vocabulary. Students are often very unimaginative when it comes to descriptions of people and they need to be directed into other ways of looking at people/families.

11.2 SB pages 74–75

Lesson plan	
Vocabulary	30–45 minutes
Grammar	20–25 minutes
Speaking	15–20 minutes
SV	Set 3 for homework.
LV	See Extension activity for 2.

Vocabulary

1 This exercise can be done using an English–English dictionary. Ask students to work in pairs.

2   Students have to think about the positive or negative meaning of the words in exercise 1, and then their opposites. Sometimes an opposite can be formed by adding a negative prefix, sometimes another word is required.

Ask students to talk about their families if there is time, using some of these adjectives. Alternatively, they could write a short piece for homework on this subject.

Extension activity

You should discuss the use of the words *funny* and *nice* in English. *Funny* can mean 'odd' or 'amusing'. It is probably safer if students avoid using *funny* for the former meaning and use *odd, strange* or *peculiar* instead. Also point out the use of *fun* rather than *funny* in the sentence: *I went to the beach and it was great fun.*

Nice is overused in both spoken and written English. Point out that there are many adjectives that can be used instead to describe a person, object or place. An awareness exercise could be done at this point.
Replace *nice* in these descriptions:
a nice vase: beautiful, old, antique, expensive, valuable
a nice old grandmother: kind, friendly, loving, dependable
nice weather: lovely, beautiful, sunny
a nice meal: delicious, tasty, well-cooked
a nice film star: handsome, good-looking, pretty, talented
a nice TV programme: interesting, absorbing, intriguing, exciting

3   Some of these phrasal verbs were in the recording in 11.1. Ask students to complete a–h with a phrasal verb or expression with *take*.

4   This section looks at a certain type of verb, usually connected with our senses. They are called copular verbs and after them we use adjectives, not adverbs.

5   The students need to compare A and B.

In A *looked* means 'seemed' or 'appeared', whereas in B *looked* means 'directed her eyes towards' – it is an action.

In A *feel* means 'experience something physical or emotional', whereas in B *felt* means 'touched' – it is an action.

Past and present participles

6   Draw students' attention to the Corpus spot. This exercise is to sort out any problems in differentiating between the use of *-ed* and *-ing*, which often causes problems for students.

Speaking

7   This provides more practice in using *-ed* and *-ing*. Check that the students know the meaning of all the adjectives.

Exam folder 6

SB pages 76–77

Paper 3 Part 1 Short extracts

Refer students to the description of Paper 3 Part 1 on page 76. It is important for students to understand that the questions test a variety of situations, functions, and types of spoken material.

1   Ask students to underline key words on their own and then compare with another student. They should underline words both in the question and in the options.

Sample answers

1   You hear a woman calling a friend.
    <u>What is she doing?</u>
    A <u>confirming</u> an <u>arrangement</u>
    B <u>complaining</u> about <u>a delay</u>
    C <u>apologising</u> for <u>her behaviour</u>

2   You hear a man and a woman talking about a film they have just seen.
    What is the man's <u>opinion</u> of the <u>film</u>?
    A It is <u>longer</u> than necessary.
    B It has a <u>weak storyline</u>.
    C Its <u>actors</u> are <u>disappointing</u>.

2   **1 17** Play the recordings and check answers at the end. Each recording is repeated, with the appropriate pauses.

Answers

1 A   2 C   3 C   4 B   5 C   6 A   7 B   8 A

Recording script

You will hear people talking in eight different situations. For questions 1–8, choose the best answer, A, B or C.
1 You hear a woman calling a friend.
Woman: Hi, Lizzie. I thought I'd just give you a ring to let you know about this afternoon. I'm actually getting an earlier flight now as I need to get to Frankfurt for a meeting at four this afternoon rather than for tomorrow morning as planned. Honestly, my boss is driving me mad – he changes plans at the drop of a hat. Anyway, <u>I hope we're still OK to meet for coffee this morning</u>. See you then. It won't take me long to get to the airport as I'm already packed.

2 You hear a man and a woman talking about a film they have just seen.
Woman: Well that was a long one, wasn't it?
Man: Was it? Seemed normal …
Woman: No, no. That scene at the end should have been cut, if you ask me. I thought Jim Franklin was really good though.
Man: Hmm, <u>I've seen him do better … and that co-star was a weak character</u>, wasn't she? What a shame – the book was absolutely gripping and they haven't changed anything, so you can't criticise the story.

3 You hear a woman describing a music festival.
Woman: It's the fifth time I've been to the festival and the programme was the best ever, with some great headline acts. They put on some excellent workshops as well, which cost us nothing – I went to one on face painting and another on African dance. I was rather disappointed that they moved the event this year, though – we had much less room than before, and the camping spots were a joke! Apart from that, we ate reasonably well even if we had to have much the same thing night after night! There were far fewer stalls to choose from this year.

4 You hear a man and a woman discussing a skiing holiday they have just been on.
Man: Well that was a great weeks skiing, wasn't it? The snow couldn't have been much better.
Woman: I suppose so but I found it quite hard dealing with those conditions for the first couple of days. I'm not quite as good at skiing as you are, remember.
Man: You did fine. What about the hotel though? I'm not sure I'd go back there again, it was a bit too big and impersonal for me, and the restaurant wasn't anything special.
Woman: Oh I don't know, the rooms were very comfortable and the pool was fantastic. For me, the only bad thing was the airline schedule, having to get up so early both ways. That was a real pain.
Man: You're right there. Well, perhaps we should take the train next time.

5 You hear this conversation in a hotel.

Receptionist: How may I help you, madam?

Woman: I was on the phone to you from my room just now and ...

Receptionist: Oh yes. There was something wrong with the phone ... Is there a problem with the room? You're in 203, aren't you?

Woman: Yes, I am ... it's fine. I was actually ringing about room service – <u>it's taken over forty minutes for them to bring me a simple sandwich and a cup of coffee</u>. Well, I was so appalled, I decided to come down here to have a word with you ...

6 You hear this radio report about a football match.

Reporter: Well, Grangewood – Trent United has finished one–nil, after a match that was full of excitement. Grangewood took the lead with Bellamy's early goal, a wonderful return for him after his long absence with that broken leg. <u>A crowd of supporters rushed across to Bellamy</u> when the game was over, glad to see their hero back. The referee tried to stop them but in the end, it was the whole Grangewood team who walked off the pitch with their delighted fans.

7 You hear part of an interview on the radio.

Interviewer: So, Duncan, you left a well-paid job in Glasgow to move to this beautiful island off the west coast of Scotland. Was it to escape the pressures of city life?

Duncan: Not really. I grew up in the countryside and I know only too well how quiet it can be – I go back to Glasgow regularly, in fact, to enjoy the fast pace again! The point is, I was trying to write a novel while I was working – you know, weekends, evenings – and I realised I couldn't do both. So I quit and <u>came here to cut costs</u> ... at the time I didn't even have a publisher's contract, so it was a risky move.

8 You hear a woman talking about an evening course.

Woman: I've started this astronomy course – two hours a week on a Monday evening. Every week the lecturer shows a short film ... we've seen one on the Hubble Space Telescope and another about the sun. It's useful, although I can't help thinking we could watch those over the Internet at home. <u>We have to work out lots of calculations in class and I must say that it's terrific!</u> I thought it would be really hard work, but the time goes by really fast and there's always a break – not that the coffee is anything special! I can't wait to get back to my sums!

3 Suggest students use a pencil to shade in the answer sheet extract. Remind them that they will have an extra five minutes in the exam to do this.

12.1

Exam skills	Speaking Paper 4 Part 2
	Reading and Use of English Paper 1 Part 7
Vocabulary	Word formation

12.2

Grammar focus	The passive
Exam skills	Reading and Use of English Paper 1 Part 4
Vocabulary	Collocations with *come*, *tell* and *fall*

Workbook contents

Reading and Use of English Paper 1 Part 5 – multiple choice

Grammar – the passive

Vocabulary – phrasal verbs with *come* and *take*

Listening Paper 3 Part 2 – sentence completion

12.1 SB pages 78–79

Lesson plan

Speaking	20–30 minutes
Reading	50–60 minutes
Vocabulary	0–10 minutes

SV Omit 3.

LV See Extension activity before and after 2.

Speaking

1   In pairs, the students should look at the photos and then answer the questions. The photos are of:

   1   a modern kitchen with many electrical appliances

   2   a woman in the early part of the last century washing clothes by hand

   3   someone travelling by sports car – quick, comfortable, exciting

   4   someone travelling by bike with a young child – 'green', healthy, economical, but possibly not as safe as a car for a child in heavy traffic

Reading

Extension activity

No dictionaries are allowed in the examination and students need to feel confident they can cope with a text without immediately reaching for their dictionary. Dictate the following sentences and ask them to work out the meaning of the words in italics (which are taken from the reading text) by thinking about the words around them. It doesn't matter if they can't come up with an exact synonym – it's the fact that they've understood what it means that counts.

a   The fashion for environmentally friendly cars only *took off* at the beginning of the twenty-first century.

b   When I got home, my shoes were really *soggy* from having to walk through the rain.

c   My sister always refuses to eat *stale* cake. She likes it straight out of the oven.

d   A neighbour *devised* a great way of cutting the grass. He got a couple of sheep to do it for him.

e   Many people are *reluctant* to put their money in that bank, after the crash.

f   The scientist was amazed by her *findings*. They didn't at all give the results that she had expected.

Answers

a   became successful/fashionable

b   wet

c   old / not fresh

d   thought of / invented / came up with

e   unwilling

f   results (of an experiment or investigation)

2   Refer the students to the Exam spot. Ask them to skim the text quickly to get an idea of what it is about and then to look at the example question. They should then move on to the complete exercise.

Answers

1 E   2 A   3 F   4 C   5 A   6 D   7 B   8 F
9 D   10 C

Extension activity

Ask students to decide which of the inventions/discoveries in the text they think has been the most significant and why.

Ask them to decide which five modern conveniences they would take to a desert island.

Vocabulary

3

Answers

a	celebrating – verb	noun: celebration
b	failed – verb	noun: failure
c	hot – adjective	noun: heat
d	fresh – adjective	noun: freshness
e	various – adjective	noun: variety
f	strong – adjective	noun: strength
g	destroying – verb	noun: destruction
h	industrial – adjective	noun: industry

12.2 SB pages 80–81

Lesson plan	
Grammar	20–25 minutes
Exam skills	10–15 minutes
Vocabulary	20–25 minutes

SV Omit 7; set 8 for homework.
LV See Extension activity after 4, 7 and 9.

The passive

1 In this exercise students have to recognise the form of the passive. They often confuse the tenses of the verb *to be* with the passive.

Answers
a active – present perfect
b past simple **passive**
c active – past simple
d present simple **passive**
e present perfect **passive**
f modal **passive**
g past perfect **passive**
h active – past simple
i present continuous **passive**
j **passive** infinitive

2 Try to elicit the answers to these questions from the students. For the formation of the passive, ask students to look in their Grammar folder, page 171. If they are still unclear, then give them a table of the tense changes.

Teaching extra

Students often worry about the formation of the passive. If they are unclear about this, put the following table on the board for them to copy down. It is important in Paper 1 Part 4 that they use the same tense as the prompt sentence, so they need to be able to manipulate active to passive and passive to active easily. Note that *get* can sometimes be used informally instead of *be*.

Present simple	*am/are/is* + past participle
Present continuous	*am/are/is being* + pp
Past simple	*was/were* + pp
Past continuous	*was/were being* + pp
Present perfect	*has/have been* + pp
Past perfect	*had been* + pp
Will	*will be* + pp
Future perfect	*will have been* + pp
Going to	*am/are/is going to be* + pp
Passive infinitive	*(to) be* + pp; *(to) have been* + pp

3 The passive is often used in newspaper reports and also to talk about processes. It is used when the action is more important than the person who is doing the action.

Answers
1 could/would be persuaded/encouraged
2 were encouraged/persuaded; have been encouraged/persuaded
3 were used
4 are (often) filled
5 can be talked into
6 are (being) supplied
7 are dissolved
8 (can be) / (are) dispersed
9 (can be) / (are) stored
10 will be issued / are going to be issued
11 is hoped
12 can be made up
13 are (constantly) being asked

4 Students often feel they need to use *by* every time they use the passive. However, it is often not needed – it can be understood.

Suggested answers
a by Spielberg.
b *correct* – (obviously by builders)
c *correct*
d *correct*
e *correct*
f deliberately / by children.

Extension activity

Students are sometimes confused about when to use *by* and when to use *with* with passive constructions. Give them the following pairs of sentences and ask them if they can work out the rule.

Shakespeare wrote Romeo and Juliet.
Romeo and Juliet was written by Shakespeare.

Money can't buy happiness.
Happiness can't be bought with money.

Elicit that in a passive clause, we usually use *by* if we want to mention the agent – the person or thing that does the action or that causes what happens. *With* is used when we talk about an instrument which is used by an agent to do an action.

Ask students to put the following sentences in the passive, using *by* and *with* as appropriate.

a Mud covered the kitchen floor.
b A cat scratched him.
c A car ran him over.
d Bulldozers smashed down the old house.
e A millionaire is giving the money to build new university accommodation.

Answers
a The kitchen floor was covered with mud.
b He was scratched by a cat.
c He was run over by a car. (we use *by* because someone was driving the car)
d The old house was smashed down *by* bulldozers. (someone was driving the bulldozers)
e New university accommodation is being built with money given by a millionaire.

5

Suggested answers
A In a canteen.
B In any public building or on public transport.
C On parking spaces or seats at a club. Somewhere where membership is important.
D On a parcel or packet of biscuits, etc.
E As a headline for a newspaper article.

Teaching extra

The passive is used in newspaper headlines, but as words are missed out, this can be very confusing to non-native speakers. Encourage students to put together articles for a class newspaper or radio programme so that they can practise using the passive in a realistic way.

6 Students should try to use the passive in their answers. In **e**, students can answer in two ways:
I was given … or *… was given to me.* The first way is neater.

7 The two pieces of information are linked in some way. Refer the students to the example.

Suggested answers
a Many watches are made in Switzerland.
b Gunpowder was invented in China.
c Tutankhamen's tomb was discovered/opened by Lord Carnarvon.
d Satellites were first sent into space in 1957.
e The 2020 Olympic Games will not be held in London.
f Togas were worn by the Romans.

Extension activity

This exercise can be extended into a game. Each team thinks of two ideas and the other team has to guess what the link is.

8 Refer students to the Exam spot. This exercise is exam practice using the passive in key word transformations. This exercise can be set for homework if time is short.

Answers
1 object to their ideas
2 were those chemicals being mixed
3 was made to hand over
4 is supposed to be
5 was informed of my boss's / his
6 would always be hidden

Corpus spot

Answers
a I was **given** a leaflet …
b … which **was built** many years ago.
c My laptop **was** bought for me two months ago.
d This brand **was** established in 1980.
e The meeting **has been** cancelled / **is** cancelled.
f It **is** located in a beautiful area.
g My friend **is** called Cecile …
h In your advertisement **it said** (that) there would be more than this.

Vocabulary

9 Students match the beginning of the sentences (a–g) with the endings (1–7).

Answers
a 5   b 4   c 1   d 6   e 7   f 3   g 2

Extension activity

Word formation
Ask students to fill in the gaps in the columns, where possible.

Noun	Person	Adjective	Verb
science			
invention			
technology			
discovery			

Answers		
Person	**Adjective**	**Verb**
scientist	scientific	–
inventor	inventive	invent
technologist/technician	technological	–
discoverer	–	discover

Writing folder 6

SB pages 82–83

Paper 2 Part 2 Reviews

1   Ask students to spend a couple of minutes listing good and bad points before discussing their ideas in pairs.

2   Suggest students focus on the adjectives in order to decide.

Answer
The writer preferred film A.

3   Ask students to skim the review to get a general idea of its meaning and then to complete gaps 1–7 on their own. They can compare their answers.

Answers
1   frighteningly realistic
2   excellent acting skills
3   interesting locations
4   fascinating storyline
5   historical events
6   shocking violence
7   tremendous soundtrack

4

Answers
a   I suggest (that) you see this film without delay.
b   *correct*
c   *correct*
d   I would advise you not to miss this film.
e   *correct*
f   I can/would recommend this film (to you).

5

Suggested answers
a   The film is directed by (Pedro Almodovar).
b   This wonderful story is set (at the end of the eighteenth century).
c   All of the costumes were designed by (students at art college).
d   The main character is played by (the French actor Daniel Auteuil).
e   The supporting cast have been chosen for (their dancing ability).
f   Most of the music was composed by (Ennio Morricone).
g   A subtitled version will be shown (in a few weeks' time).
h   The screenplay has just been nominated for (an award).

6   Give students a minute to read the exam question.

7   Suggest students brainstorm the nouns in groups.

Possible answers
comedy: jokes, comedian, laughter, humour
documentary: photography, wildlife, facts, interviews
game show: quiz, questions, points, prize
reality show: celebrities, relationships, lifestyle, conflict
soap opera: drama, script, character, plot, story

8   Ask students to develop a paragraph plan. The review can be written for homework, using the one in 3 as a model.

Sample answer
One of my favourite shows on TV is the comedy series *Frasier*, starring Kelsey Grammer. Although new programmes are no longer being made of this long-running series, it is possible to watch regular repeats.

The key to the programme's success is the sensitive and humorous way in which it shows everyday life. Frasier hosts a radio phone-in show, assisted by his efficient producer Roz Doyle. The supporting cast includes his father Martin, a retired policeman, who lives with Frasier; Martin's amusing (and exceptionally well-trained) dog Eddie; Frasier's younger brother Niles, who has gone through many disappointments in love and yet who finally ends up with the woman of his dreams, Daphne Moon; and Frasier's icy ex-wife Lilith and their son Freddy, who appear on the programme from time to time.

The series is set in Seattle and rarely strays far from this city. In fact, the two commonest locations are Frasier's apartment and his broadcasting room at the radio station. But the programmes are never dull! What makes this series so remarkable is its scripts, which are tightly written and contain some memorable jokes. I highly recommend this show.

(190 words)

Units 7–12 Revision

SB pages 84–85

Lesson plan

Grammar	15–15 minutes
Topic review	15–35 minutes
Vocabulary	15–15 minutes
Phrasal verbs	0–10 minutes
Writing	15 minutes

SV   Set Phrasal verbs as homework.
LV   Extend Topic review (see 2).

Grammar

1   This picture shows Kim Basinger in the film *LA Confidential*.

Answers
1 in   **2** although/though/while/whilst
3 must/would/might/could   **4** be
5 All/Most   **6** a   **7** because   **8** This/It

Topic review

2   Follow the procedure given for Units 1–6 (see page 38).

Extension activity

Ask students to write one or two sentences each, based on some of the six topics in Units 7–12. They should then discuss them in groups.

Vocabulary

3   The verbs are *get* and *take*.

Answers
a getting   **b** takes   **c** get   **d** getting   **e** take
f got   **g** take   **h** take

4   Stress that students must explain why each word they choose is the odd one out. Give them an example if necessary:

a   I think *cunning* is the odd one out because it means 'clever'. The other three words all refer to something bad, like a frightening experience.

Suggested answers
a cunning (clever; the other three refer to something bad)
b campaign (an advertising campaign involves many activities; the other three are features of advertisements)
c snowboarding (this is a sport which is usually done outside; the others normally take place inside)
d fancy (means that you like someone or something; the other three verbs mean the opposite)
e shallow ('shallow' describes a small depth, whereas the other adjectives refer to large dimensions)
f sports centre (you can find the other three at a sports centre)
g pretend (deceive; the other three refer to the future in some way)
h extravagant (spending more than is necessary; the other three refer to spending less)

Phrasal verbs

5   If this is done in class, suggest that students complete the sentences on their own and then compare their answers in pairs.

Answers
a looked   **b** get   **c** kept   **d** switching
e take   **f** work   **g** put   **h** broke

Writing

6   Give students time to read through the paragraphs and then suggest that they work in groups, discussing the different styles for 1–4.

Answers
A 4 (conclusion)   **B** 2   **C** 3 (opening)

13.1

Exam skills	Speaking Paper 4 Part 2
Listening	Reporting verbs
Vocabulary	Word formation
	Collocations

13.2

Grammar focus	Reporting
Exam skills	Listening Paper 3 Part 3
Grammar extra	Reported questions
Exam skills	Speaking Paper 4 Part 3
Exam skills	Reading and Use of English Paper 1 Part 4

Workbook contents

Reading and Use of English Paper 1 Part 6 – gapped text
Grammar – reported speech
Vocabulary – phrases with *make*

13.1 SB pages 86–87

Lesson plan

Speaking	20–30 minutes
Listening	20 minutes
Vocabulary	30–40 minutes

SV	Omit 7 and 9 or set as written homework.
LV	Allow more time for discussion in 7.

This lesson gives plenty of opportunities for students to use reported speech, which will be familiar to most of them. Although they should be aware of the tenses they are using, don't introduce any grammatical explanation in this lesson; 13.2 will focus on this.

Speaking

1 Allow students about five minutes to compare the photographs and make a brief reference to their own experience.

Background information
Since 2013, it is compulsory for children to attend school in Britain between the ages of 5 and 18. There are both state and private schools. For younger children, some nursery education is offered by the state and the government has promised more money for this; there is a large private nursery sector.

2 Allow students around six to eight minutes for this paired discussion, reminding them to listen carefully and take notes if necessary, so that they can report later. Be ready to help with vocabulary.

In the report stage, ask different pairs to report the information in a–d. Encourage students to vary the reporting verbs they use and write some of their sentences on the board. Underline the tenses used and elicit what they are.

3 If this is to be done in class, ask students to first read David's confession on their own. Then they can rewrite it on their own or in pairs, taking it in turns to do a sentence each. Check the finished piece of writing by asking a student to read it aloud, or take all copies in for marking.

Answer
David said that he wanted to describe what had really happened. He had been inside the classroom during break and he had seen a group of his friends outside. He had gone over to the window and (had) tried to get their attention. He had waved at them but they hadn't seen him, so he had hammered on the window. He said he knew glass was/is* breakable but he just hadn't thought. When his hand had gone through, he had panicked. He hadn't been badly hurt and he had wanted to avoid getting into trouble, so he had put Simon's bag over the hole and had left the room. He said he was sorry he hadn't told anyone the truth until then / that moment.
* Because it is a fact that glass is breakable, the present tense can also be used here.

Listening

4 **2 02** This listening exercise focuses on paraphrase and meaning. There is an exam training exercise in 13.2.

Ask students to read the eight statements. Elicit key words in each statement and check understanding, for example, *deliberately* in **b** and *irritating* in **c**. Explain that the recording is full-length and may contain some difficult words, as in the exam. Play it straight through the first time. If students have problems when they compare answers, split the piece up the second time and reinforce where each answer comes (see underlinings in recording script).

Answers
a T   b T   c F   d F   e T   f T   g F   h T

Recording script

Interviewer: With me now are Sandra Wilson and Mike Tripp. Mike is owner of a successful new travel company, Just Trips, and Sandra works for him as Publicity Manager. They were actually in the same class at school, though at that time, they did *not* get on with each other! They met again by chance last year, when Sandra went for an interview at Just Trips and was surprised to find Mike across the table. Sandra, when you were at school, did you think Mike would become successful like this?

Sandra: To be honest, no one thought Mike would get anywhere – <u>he was the original under-achiever!</u> <u>That's why we didn't get on.</u> My group of friends were quite hard-working – you know, we did all the homework, made an effort in class – but Mike was the complete opposite. <u>He was bad news, actually.</u>

Interviewer: Is this true, Mike?

Mike: I'm afraid so. I wasn't the only one though. It was ... uncool for boys to work, a whole group of us were like that. I don't remember being especially horrible to Sandra ...

Sandra: <u>Talk about a selective memory!</u>

Interviewer: Why?

Sandra: Well, he would regularly do annoying things like stealing my ruler or hiding my books. You saw it as a big joke, I suppose, Mike?

Mike: Never thought about it. <u>I can see now that I might have been a bit ... a bit of a nuisance.</u>

Sandra: I've forgiven you though!

Interviewer: And you've done very well since, Mike ...

Mike: Yeah. I got on with my life. Um ... <u>I don't really regret my behaviour back then</u> – obviously I shouldn't have made trouble for you, Sandra – but for myself, it didn't matter ... <u>I've done OK in spite of school.</u>

Sandra: You have, Mike, but there are lots of others in your gang who didn't make it.

Mike: Mmm ... I can think of one or two ... But I still think, if you know what you want out of life, you'll get there. I mean, look at me, I didn't pass many exams ... <u>I even walked out of some, like science ... wrote my name at the top of the paper and thought, I can't do this</u> ... oh, what the heck, the sun's shining, I'm off.

Sandra: Incredible! I was totally stressed out during exams, spent hours revising, and Mike managed to fail virtually everything and still be successful.

Interviewer: Should you have been more relaxed at school, Sandra?

Sandra: That's easy to say now. I had a lot of pressure on me to do well. My parents, my brothers ... all my family expected ... the best.

Mike: <u>Same here. But my dad sort of looked beyond school. He knew I'd be OK – he'd left school himself at 14 and he always felt that I'd sort things out for myself, somehow.</u>

Interviewer: And how *did* you get the company started? No careers advice from school, I imagine?

Mike: <u>Careers teachers? They didn't have a clue!</u> I got things started in a small way while I was still at school, actually – I used to help out in a local travel agency, buying and selling cheap tickets on the phone. In my final year, I sometimes spent my lunchtimes checking the internet on the school computer. I found some good deals for flights, that I managed to sell on. Then, <u>when I left school, my dad gave me a bit of money and I set up an office</u> ... and it all ... like ... took off.

Interviewer: So school did help you a little ... or its facilities did?

Mike: Yeah ...

Interviewer: OK, well we'll have to leave it there. One final thing, Mike. Why did Sandra get the job?

Mike: Oh, university education, languages, a good communicator – she's great, just what the company needed.

Sandra: All thanks to school, Mike.

Vocabulary

5   Encourage students to think in terms of word families, as this will help them to extend their vocabulary knowledge.

Answers
a educate   b educated   c educational

6   Note that these are some of the most frequent collocates for *educational* and *educated*.

Answers
educational + qualifications, opportunities, standards (a, c, d)
educated + person (b)

The adjective *educational* is much **more** frequent than *educated* and can be used with a number of noun collocates. The ones included in this exercise are among the most frequent collocations for *educational*. *Educated* is used to describe people and can be qualified by an adverb or noun or proper noun, for example *highly/well educated, university educated, Harvard educated*, etc.

7 These sentences are taken from past exam answers and include some relevant vocabulary: *motivation, reward, results, discipline, methods, rules*. Allow students five to ten minutes to discuss their ideas in groups.

8 Ask students to look at the photos before they read the six texts. Explain that some answers are easier to work out than others and suggest that students look for clues in the texts.

> **Answers**
> **A** Tom Cruise   **B** Paul Gauguin   **C** Annie Lennox
> **D** Socrates   **E** Madonna   **F** Agatha Christie

9 If done in class, try to have some English–English dictionaries on hand. The next Writing folder is after Unit 14, on pages 96–97. Useful words and phrases include:
(A) earn/make in a day
(B) have (a) talent for, determination
(C) On leaving school …, find employment
(D) gain experience, spend x years …, full-time career
(E) work long hours
(F) take a position, unpaid assistant, qualify in, duties, a sound knowledge of, extremely relevant

13.2 SB pages 88–89

> **Lesson plan**
> Grammar   20–30 minutes
> Listening   25–35 minutes
> Grammar extra   5–10 minutes
> Use of English   15 minutes
>
> **SV**   Set study of Grammar folder in 1 and exercise in Grammar extra for homework; keep 8 brief.
> **LV**   See Extension activity for 3 and notes for 8.

Reporting

1 Ask students to look at the three quotes in pairs and discuss the tenses used. They should then look at the Grammar folder, page 171.

> **Answers**
> In **a**, there is 'backshift' in the reported statement. Greg's actual statement contained a present and a future tense; in reported speech, the present tense *can't* has become a past tense *couldn't*, and *will* has become *would*.
>
> In **b**, there is similar backshift from the past simple to the past perfect in the reported statement.
>
> In **c**, the reported statement uses the present because the situation reported continues to be true.

2 Ask students to do the exercise on their own and then compare their answers.

> **Answers**
> **a** 3   **b** 4   **c** 1   **d** 2

3 Explain to students that there are a number of reporting verbs in English. Using a variety of these in Paper 2 Writing will impress the examiner, particularly if the structures following the verbs are correct. Draw students' attention to the Corpus spot.

Further useful verbs which could be given to students are:
encourage: encourage + someone + to + infinitive
threaten: threaten + someone + with + something; threaten + to + infinitive; threaten + that (optional)

> **Answers**
> apologise (+ to someone) + for + -ing e.g. *She apologised (to me) for forgetting my birthday.*
> argue + for/against + noun or -ing; argue + that e.g. *The students argued against wearing school uniform / argued that school uniforms were unnecessary.*
> claim + that (optional) e.g. *He claimed (that) the river had been polluted by factory waste.*
> deny + that (optional); deny + -ing e.g. *She denied (that) she had taken the money. / She denied taking the money.*
> explain (+ to someone) + that (optional) e.g. *We explained (to them) (that) we had lost their phone number.*
> insist + on + -ing; insist + that (optional) e.g. *They insisted on paying for our lunch. / They insisted (that) they wouldn't leave without seeing the manager.*
> promise (+ someone) + that (optional); promise + to infinitive e.g. *She promised (me) (that) she would write to me every day. / She promised to write to me every day.*
> refuse + to infinitive e.g. *I refused to listen to his excuses.*
> say + that (optional); in passive, 'is said' + to infinitive e.g. *He said that he needed a holiday. / He is said to be one of the world's greatest athletes.*
> suggest + that (optional); suggest + -ing e.g. *They suggested (that) we meet at the café. / They suggested meeting at the café.*
> urge + someone + to infinitive; urge + that e.g. *I urged him to tell his parents.*
> warn (+ someone) + that (optional); + (not) to infinitive e.g. *I warned them (that) it was dangerous to swim here. / I warned them not to swim here.*

Extension activity

Develop this work into a dictionary session, where students find examples to illustrate each of the structures.

Listening

4   Refer students to the Exam spot and elicit predictions from the class.

5   **2 03** Play the recording of Speaker 1 and ask students to complete the summary.

Answers
1 are   **2** need   **3** are affected
Speaker 1: statement F

Recording script
Speaker 1: I'm a retired head teacher and I want to make two points. First, I know from my own experience that teachers <u>tend to be</u> female ... and I believe we need to get more men into all our schools – boys need men around as role models, from an early age. My second point is linked to this. There is a growing problem of broken marriages and one-parent families, which affects all children but especially boys, because they usually end up living with their mothers and having less contact with their fathers. Men are so important to boys' development.

6   **2 04** Listen to the rest of the recording. Ask students to summarise the main points. If time is short, move straight to the answers.

Suggested answers
Speaker 2: statement E
She said that when boys and girls start school, they are both keen to learn.
She complained that parents don't help boys at home.
She insisted that basic skills have to be introduced in the home.

Speaker 3: statement A
He suggested discussing society rather than just schools.
He explained that as society has changed so much, boys don't have clear goals any more.
He claimed that girls, in contrast, have a lot to aim for.

Speaker 4: statement H
She explained that girls' brains develop differently to boys' at a young age.
She warned that in Britain education is too formal at the beginning.
She urged that nursery education should be extended to the age of six in Britain.

Speaker 5: statement B
He insisted on the recent achievement by girls being seen as a good thing.
He argued that this was not true ten years ago.
He suggested that this is part of more equal opportunities nowadays.

Recording script
Speaker 2: Well, I'm an infant teacher and I work with children from the age of four. Both boys and girls arrive at school interested and excited on day one. But I find during that first year that I can't get the parents of boys to help their children at home. They expect their boys to be out playing football after school, not sitting at home reading a book. Basic skills have to be introduced in the home, and because the girls' parents do this, the girls <u>race ahead</u>. Then the boys feel they're failing, so they start <u>mucking about</u>, and things go from bad to worse.

Speaker 3: Can I widen the topic beyond schools? Society has changed radically in the last twenty years and fathers are no longer the <u>bread-winners</u>, necessarily. Indeed, the average boy growing up now may see a lot of men who are unemployed ... and of course he's going to look at that and say, 'What's the point? There's no future for me.' Girls, on the other hand, now see lots of opportunities and they want to get out there and compete, get to the top. We haven't <u>faced up to</u> this, and yet it was obviously going to happen.

Speaker 4: <u>Picking up on</u> what the infant teacher said, I've always understood the brain develops differently in boys and girls, so girls aged four develop quickly, whereas boys take longer to get going. For boys especially, I think we formalise education too soon in Britain. I can find no other examples in the world where formal teaching starts so early. I believe we should <u>extend</u> nursery education to the age of six, so that there is more time for play, for discovery ... and above all, language. Then by the age of six, boys would be ready for formal learning.

Speaker 5: I think we should <u>give credit to</u> what has happened ... I mean, it's a success story for girls, isn't it? OK, so girls are now achieving better results at school than boys ... which is great. It was not the case twenty years ago ... even ten years ago. For the last three years, more girls have gained university places than boys ... good for them. I think this is all part of the wider picture of equal opportunities and we should view it positively.

7   Play the recording again and ask students to note down the relevant words and phrases.

Answers
a tend (to be)   **b** race ahead   **c** mucking about
d bread-winners   **e** faced up to   **f** picking up on
g extend   **h** give credit to

Grammar extra

Draw attention to the changes in word order in the examples. The exercise can be done in class or for homework.

Answers
a why girls are/were gaining more university places.
b in what ways the situation had been different twenty years ago.
c if/whether things would get better in the future.
d if/whether British children should spend more time at nursery school.
e why we hadn't faced up to this problem.

8 Refer students to the question in bold and the five groups, which indicate the different people and institutions that have responsibility for a child's education. Explain that in the exam, they will need to address all five ideas that are shown over the two minutes. The examiner will then stop their discussion and give them a further minute to decide on two out of the five, as in exercise 9.

Possible answers
Parents could spend more time reading to young children and encouraging older ones to focus on their homework.

Teachers might offer extra lessons free of charge after school, or attend professional development workshops.

The media could support educational initiatives and publicise examples of best practice.

The government might spend more money upgrading schools and increase teachers' salaries.

Local companies could fund special projects at their local schools or invite students on work experience programmes.

9 Encourage students to use phrases like *On the one hand … On the other hand* when discussing which two groups to choose. They should either reach agreement on their choices, or agree to disagree.

10

Answers
1 accused Charlie of putting
2 warned Johnny not to misbehave / warned Johnny to stop misbehaving
3 urged them not to fall
4 (that) she had not / hadn't wasted
5 if/whether they had tidied up
6 apologised for forgetting

Exam folder 7

SB pages 90–91

Paper 3 Part 3
Multiple matching

Ask students to read through the introduction and the Advice box. Each extract they hear lasts about 30 seconds.

1 **2 05** Students need to look at the statements A–H very carefully. One wrong answer could affect two answers.

Let them have a good look at the statements and check they understand any vocabulary. Ask them to cover up the extract from the recording script and the analysis which follows. Play the recording, then check they have B as the answer.

They should then read through the recording script and look at the analysis of the questions.

Recording script

You will hear the first speaker talking about his experience of education. Look at the statements A–H and decide which one is true for the first speaker.

Speaker 1: When I started my last year at school, I didn't take it seriously enough. <u>I should've chosen subjects which were useful rather than ones I liked or that sounded easy.</u> By the time the exams came, I'd given up and I did very badly. I knew I'd have to work hard but I wasn't able to catch up with my friends. Because I failed at science, I can't be a teacher, which is what I really want to do. I'm doing a part-time job in order to make ends meet and next year I'll be starting evening classes to get better qualifications.

---

2 **2 06** Play the rest of the recording for questions 2–5. Ask the students to cover the recording script.

Answers
2 F   3 D   4 H   5 A

Recording script

Speaker 2: I left school and moved to a college to take my final exams. It was the best decision I could have made. <u>At the college nobody seemed to care about homework and this really motivated me. I had to plan my work myself – there was no one to make you do it and no one to check up on what you'd done.</u> I was still dependent on my parents for money – but that was OK. I learned a lot about real life there – things like getting on with people and organising your time, which has been really useful now I'm working.

Speaker 3: When I left school, I didn't have a particular career in mind so I decided to do Environmental Studies at university, mainly because I'd enjoyed geography at school. I didn't really like the course at university and I did think about leaving, but instead I changed courses, which was easier than I expected. I think university was useful in that I learnt how to live alone and <u>how to budget, and as I'm an underpaid teacher now, that really helps</u>.

Speaker 4: I had no difficulty choosing what I was going to do – my parents are both doctors and ever since I was small I also wanted to do that. They really encouraged me and I did well at school and got into a good medical school fairly easily. <u>It was surprisingly tough at medical school</u>, but I had some good friends and we pulled through together. I think the doubts only began to set in when I graduated and got my first job in a hospital. I began to wonder if I'd missed out because I'd been so focused on becoming a doctor. So now I'm doing some voluntary work in Africa, which I'm really enjoying.

Speaker 5: I decided to take a year off after doing my last year at school. I'd had enough of revising and sitting in a library, so I decided to go off to Australia for nine months and earn a bit of money. I've got relatives there who put me up when I first arrived and found me a job. It wasn't doing anything particularly interesting, <u>but the great part was that I was getting to know people who were completely different to the ones I'd known back home</u>. I really recommend taking a year out, but you need to have a firm plan or it could end up a waste of time.

3 Students should now look at the recording script and underline the parts which gave them the answer.

14 Career moves

14.1

Exam skills	Speaking Paper 4 Part 2
	Reading and Use of English Paper 1 Part 7
Vocabulary	Word formation: negative prefixes
Grammar extra	*all / the whole*

14.2

Grammar focus	Perfect tenses
Listening and role play	Job interviews

Workbook contents

Reading and Use of English Paper 1 Part 3 – word formation
Listening Paper 3 Part 1 – short extracts
Writing Paper 2 Part 1 – essay
Grammar – *all / the whole*

14.1 SB pages 92–93

Lesson plan

Speaking	15–25 minutes
Reading	25 minutes
Vocabulary	20 minutes
Grammar extra	10–20 minutes

SV Keep discussion in 1 brief; set Grammar extra exercise for homework.
LV See Extension activity for 2.

Speaking

1 Suggest that students work in pairs, each talking about one of the jobs shown. These are: a restorer of ancient pottery and a member of a Formula One technical support team. Skills needed include precision, patience, specialised knowledge of archaeology, steady hands, good eyesight, self-motivation (restorer); quick-thinking, physical strength, ability to work under pressure, being a team player (Formula One).

Elicit opinions from the class on the final question: Which job would you prefer and why? This is an example of what happens at the end of a 'long turn' in Paper 4 Part 2, where the candidate who has been listening makes a brief comment. Students will be introduced to a full Paper 4 Part 2 in Unit 17.

2 Some of these words come up in the article which follows. Ask students to complete the quotes and then elicit the meaning of the other words.

> **Answers**
> **a** secure   **b** flexible; adventurous   **c** concerned

Extension activity

If more time is available, divide the class into four teams and allocate one of the changes below to each team, asking them to discuss the advantages and disadvantages of the change. They should prepare their ideas on a flip chart, overhead transparency or presentation slide, to present to the class.

Other changes in the job market include:
- growing computerisation and automation, causing job losses
- outsourcing of work to other parts of the world where labour costs are lower, leading to downsizing of the original staff
- increasing number of freelance workers
- more employees working remotely from home.

Reading

3 Refer students to the Exam spot and stress that, because of the number of items and the length of the text, they must scan for the information rather than read word by word.

Ask students to read through the questions and think about key words to look out for in the article. They should then complete the task within ten minutes, and compare answers.

> **Answers**
> **1** A   **2** B   **3** D   **4** E   **5** C   **6** A   **7** D   **8** D
> **9** C   **10** E

4 These questions are to raise awareness of negative prefixes. Ask students to work through them in pairs and then elicit their ideas.

> **Possible answers**
> **a** She had been doing the job for too long; her life felt empty outside work; she was getting fed up with the travelling.
> **b** She wouldn't have been familiar with the latest equipment/machinery; she wouldn't have been able to handle the financial side of farming.
> **c** She doesn't have a regular salary; she works irregular hours.

Vocabulary

5

> **Answers**
> **a** disorganised   **b** impatient   **c** unsuccessful
> **d** dishonest   **e** irresponsible

Grammar extra

Explain that *all* is a very common word in English and is used in many useful expressions. Ask students to look at a–h in pairs and elicit answers.

> **Answers**
> **a** = had everything   **b** *used for emphasis*
> **c** = from the beginning
> **d** *used with a superlative for emphasis*
> **e** = suddenly   **f** = despite
> **g** = on balance; *used to summarise after different things have been considered*   **h** = more than anything

Refer students to the example and its use of *whole*. Explain that sometimes it is possible to use both *all* and *(the) whole*, although other words may have to be added to *all* to make the expression fit grammatically. For example, you can say *all the class bought the book / all of the class bought the book / the whole class bought the book* but if you use *all* with a pronoun, you must use *of*, as in *all of us bought the book*.

> **Answers**
> **1** all (of the)   **2** the whole (of the)   **3** The whole (of the)
> **4** all   **5** all / the whole; all of   **6** all (of)

Encourage students to work out the rules, suggesting they think about the words which follow *all* and *whole*:
- Are the nouns singular or plural?
- What other words have they used? (*of the*)
- What words can come before *whole*? Remind them of the example: *my whole life*.
- Elicit also the meaning of *On the whole ...*

Refer them to the Grammar folder, page 172 afterwards.

Teaching extra

For some areas of common error, like *all / the whole*, students need to be reminded of the correct form or usage more than once. In a spare five minutes at the end of a lesson, try giving students a set of sentences which pick up on a previous grammar point. The sentences should be a mix of correct and incorrect ones, with students being asked to make the necessary corrections. Below is an example for *all / the whole*, which you could use in a fortnight's time.
1 Jack's whole life has been spent worrying about money.
2 All you must listen to what I'm saying.
3 My all plan for the future has gone wrong.
4 The police have warned the company to check all postal packages.
5 The whole drinks should be kept cool.

> **Answers**
> **1** ✓   **2** All of you ...   **3** My whole plan ...
> **4** ✓   **5** All (of) the drinks

14.2 SB pages 94–95

Lesson plan	
Grammar	20 minutes
Listening	15 minutes
Role play	20–30 minutes
Grammar	15–25 minutes

SV   Limit role play to one turn in 5.
LV   See Extension activity for 6.

Perfect tenses

1   Ask students to discuss the differences in meaning and identify the tenses used in pairs. Elicit responses.

> **Answers**
> Sentence **a** says that the person has sent no emails (neither in the past nor in the present).
> Sentence **b** only refers to the past and doesn't tell us whether the situation is still true.
> Sentence **c** tells us that the person started to send emails at some point in the past but before that time had never sent any.
> Sentence **d** forecasts a future situation at a certain time.
> **a** present perfect
> **b** past simple
> **c** past perfect; past simple
> **d** future perfect

2   Allow students around six minutes for this task. All the examples come from the article in 14.1. If they need extra context, they can look back at this.

> **Answers**
> **1** b   **2** f, h   **3** h   **4** c, e, a   **5** a   **6** g   **7** d
> The future perfect continuous tense has not been exemplified. Example: *John will have been driving a taxi for thirteen years next April.*

3   Refer students to the Grammar folder, page 172, before they do this exercise.

> **Answers**
> **a** have been showing
> **b** was voted
> **c** has been studying
> **d** will have been working
> **e** had feared
> **f** will have been launched
> **g** has made
> **h** had been waiting

Corpus spot

Answers

a I felt very sorry after I **had seen** your report.
b Some months ago he **directed** a movie.
c *correct*
d For thousands of years our civilisation **has been making** progress.
e When I left your house in Ljubljana, I **decided** to visit the lakes.
f Some friends of mine **were working** there last summer.
g *correct*
h The Astrid Hotel **has been closed** since last year.

Listening

4 **2 07** Play the recording and ask students to note down the relevant words and phrases for skills and qualities in each extract. Pause after each one to review answers.

Answers
Speaker 1 (office administrator): flexible; (have) commitment; not mind working long hours
Speaker 2 (interpreter): keen on languages; speaks three languages; fluent; dealing with people face to face; a talent for communication; think really fast; confidence; positive person
Speaker 3 (shop assistant): dress well; know a lot about ...; handle pressure
Speaker 4 (first-aid worker): get a first-aid qualification; (have) lots of energy; extremely fit; specialise in
Speaker 5 (cook): cope with working at speed; being better organised; staying in control

Recording script
Speaker 1: There's a big music festival in my town every summer. For the last three years, I've worked in the festival office, doing a whole range of things, from putting leaflets in envelopes to arranging hotel bookings for the various performers. I know I'm <u>flexible</u> – I've had to be – and I've definitely <u>got commitment</u> – <u>I don't mind working long hours</u> as long as there's an end in sight! I really enjoy big events, too – the more people there are, the more enjoyable it is!

Speaker 2: I've always been <u>interested in languages</u>. My mother's from Quebec in Canada, so we <u>speak both German and French</u> at home. I've been <u>learning English</u> since I was 12. By next summer, I'll have been learning it for over ten years, so I'm sure I'll be really <u>fluent</u>. I like <u>dealing with people face to face</u> and people say I've got quite a lot of <u>talent for communication</u>. I can <u>think really fast</u>, which gives

me <u>a lot of confidence</u>. Oh, and I'm a very <u>positive person</u> too!

Speaker 3: I've been working in The Gap since I left college last year. I think I <u>dress well</u> myself – that's important when you're in this sort of job. I <u>know a lot about</u> sports and leisure clothing, and I often get asked for advice when people are choosing what to buy. Once you've worked in a busy clothing store you can <u>handle anything</u> – I <u>don't mind pressure</u>, in fact it's usually a good thing – makes the day go more quickly.

Speaker 4: I'm having a year off between school and medical school. At the moment I'm doing part-time voluntary work in a hospital. I've also been going to evening classes to <u>get a first-aid qualification</u>, which I've just managed to get. <u>I've got lots of energy</u> and I like to think I'm <u>extremely fit</u>. My boyfriend thinks I'm obsessed with sport, actually – I swim for a club and I play tennis or basketball whenever I get the chance. I'd like to <u>specialise in</u> sports medicine when I'm older.

Speaker 5: I did a one-year course in catering after leaving school, and since then I've been working alongside one of Edinburgh's top chefs. She's taught me so much – not just recipes and techniques, either. The most important thing I've learned is how to <u>cope with working at speed</u>. It can get very busy some evenings, but through her, I've developed ways of <u>being better organised</u> ... er ... <u>staying in control</u> when it gets really hot in the kitchen.

Now write the five jobs as headings on the board and elicit other useful skills and qualifications for each one, in preparation for the role play.

5 Explain that the role play involves attending an interview for one of the five jobs. Student A is the interviewee and Student B is the interviewer. A variation on this would be to set up groups of four, consisting of a panel of interviewers and one interviewee, but this may be too daunting for some students!

Allow students about four minutes to read their instructions and prepare what they are going to say. Student B should decide which job is on offer and think of questions to ask.

Allow students about five minutes for the first turn and then, if you have time, suggest they swap roles.

At the end, ask some of the interviewers to report their views to the class, based on the criteria and scale of 0–5. Tell students that the language they have used will be extremely useful in Writing folder 7, which is on applications.

6 Ask students to skim the article and decide who it is written for (office workers). Then ask them to work through the article on their own, filling in gaps 1–12 with the correct tense. Remind them that they must use perfect tenses. The past or present simple may sometimes appear possible, but what is asked for is a perfect tense: present, past or future perfect, simple or continuous, active or passive.

Answers
1 have shrunk   2 has brought   3 have been set up
4 has been growing   5 have ceased   6 have become
7 have been putting in   8 have shown   9 has found
10 will have been given   11 will have been claiming
12 have rambled on / have been rambling on

Extension activity

Ask students, in pairs or small groups, to discuss the five pieces of advice and to decide which are the three most important. They should give reasons for their views. Elicit opinions at the end.

DO YOU WANT TO CHECK STUDENT PROGRESS?
PROGRESS TEST 7 ON THE TEACHER'S RESOURCES CD-ROM

Writing folder 7

SB pages 96–97

Paper 2 Part 2
Letters of Application

Letters of application appear in Paper 2 Part 2. They are usually presented in the form of an advertisement for a job.

1 Many of these words have come up already in Units 13 and 14. Ask students to write the adjectives related to these nouns.

Answers
motivated   committed   determined   cheerful
enthusiastic   energetic   organised   talented
skilled/skilful   confident

2 In pairs, ask students to discuss the qualities and skills needed. Remind them to think about the whole content of the advert, i.e. the introductory text and all three bulleted points. They should put themselves in the position of the target reader and decide what information the company would need in order to make a decision about an applicant.

3 Ask students to discuss the two letters and decide whether both have covered everything.

Answer
Letter A has covered all the points.
Letter B has omitted to talk about his knowledge of English. The letter is thin on relevant experience and on the reason why he would like the job. It is also thin on personal qualities and what is said would probably irritate the reader. The letter is also inappropriately informal and its tone is too colloquial/chatty.

4 Suggest students rewrite the letter in pairs, discussing their improvements. Refer them to the Exam advice.

5 Ask students to read the task and underline the key points.

They should answer all three bulleted questions, including some reference to the qualities needed (*energetic* and *cheerful*). For a high mark, there should also be a mention of where they saw the advertisement.

Encourage students to make a paragraph plan and remind them not to include postal addresses in their answers.

Sample answer
Dear Sir or Madam

I am writing to apply for the job of tour guide with Europewide Coach Tours, which was advertised in 'The Times' last Saturday. I am just the person you are looking for.

I have been studying English for twelve years, so I am fluent. I recently spent three months in London, as part of my studies. I also speak French and a little German.

Although I know many parts of Europe well, I am always keen to visit new places and find out more about them. It would be good to share this knowledge with others.

People say I am a good communicator and I enjoy being with other people. I have a good sense of humour and plenty of energy.

In terms of relevant experience, I have spent the last two summers working as a guide, taking groups of foreign tourists on walking tours around our city. I therefore have a good understanding of the needs of visitors from other countries.

I hope you will consider my application favourably.

Yours faithfully

15 Too many people?

15.1

Exam skills	Speaking Paper 4 Parts 2 and 4 Listening Paper 3 Part 2
Vocabulary	Topic set – the natural world Word formation
Exam skills	Reading and Use of English Paper 1 Part 3
Speaking	Saying numbers and letters

15.2

Grammar focus	Countable and uncountable nouns *some, any, no*
Vocabulary	Expressions of quantity
Exam skills	Reading and Use of English Paper 1 Part 2

Workbook contents

Reading and Use of English Paper 1 Part 1 – multiple choice cloze
Vocabulary – the environment
Writing – linkers, informal letter
Grammar – *some, any, no, every*

15.1 SB pages 98–99

Lesson plan

Speaking	10–15 minutes
Listening	15–20 minutes
Vocabulary	15–25 minutes
Speaking	15–25 minutes

SV	Omit 4; set 5 for homework.
LV	See Extension activity for 8.

Speaking

1 **The photos show**
  1 tourists climbing up the Pyramid of the Sun (Piramide del Sol), Teotihuacan Archaeological Site, Mexico
  2 Stonehenge, UK, where tourists are not allowed to touch the stone circle, but must view it from a short distance away
  3 tourists in St Mark's Square, Venice
  4 a Nepalese sherpa collecting garbage, left by climbers, at an altitude of 8,000 metres during the Everest clean-up expedition at Mount Everest. (In 2010 a group of 20 Nepalese climbers braved thin air and below freezing temperatures in a high-risk expedition to clear around two tonnes of rubbish left behind by mountaineers.)

Listening

2 **2 08 A woman is talking about the problems faced by the Grand Canyon National Park Service. Students have to complete the notes. There are more answers relating to numbers than there would be in Listening Part 2 in the exam. This is for practice purposes.**

> **Answers**
> 1 northwestern   2 1.6 kms / kilometres   3 1919
> 4 5m / million   5 free buses   6 air pollution
> 7 water   8 7 / seven degrees   9 fish
> 10 (seven/7 natural) wonders

> ### Recording script
> **Presenter:** Situated in the <u>northwestern</u> part of Arizona, the Grand Canyon is one of the natural wonders of the world. Contrary to popular belief, the Grand Canyon is not the longest, deepest or widest canyon in the world. But it is accessible, and with little vegetation to hide it, it feels big. Nothing prepares you for that first sight of it. From the top it drops <u>1.6 kilometres</u> to the desert floor below. But however vast it seems, it is not big enough to support the millions of people who visit it every year.
>
> When one section of the Grand Canyon was declared a national park in <u>1919</u>, three years after the creation of the National Park Service, visitor numbers were 44,000. Today, with <u>five million</u> visitors a year, the Park Service is finding it difficult to keep the Canyon accessible to the public and to safeguard it for future generations.
>
> The pressures on the Grand Canyon National Park forced the Park Service to draw up a management plan. One of the first problems it tackled was that of the large number of visitors' cars which needed parking space. The Park Service got around the problem by allowing visitors to take advantage of <u>free buses</u>, which take them on a number of routes around the park.
>
> Some of the other problems faced by the park are the result of things happening outside its boundaries. Take <u>air pollution</u>. On summer days, when there are southwesterly winds, the pollution blown in from Southern California can restrict the views over the Canyon.
>
> Then, another of the big problems is the availability of water resources in the park, as, at present, there is a drought. The Park cannot draw water from the

river but only from a spring on the north side of the canyon, using a pipeline. If this pipeline is damaged, then <u>water</u> has to be brought in by truck. This last happened in 1995 when floods caused a landslide, which destroyed the pipeline.

The Colorado river, which created the Canyon, looks wild but in fact is managed intensely. Twenty-four kilometres upstream is the Glen Canyon Dam, which has had a profound impact on the river. Now the river flow is about a tenth of what it was previously.

The Colorado used to reach temperatures of 24 degrees in summer. Today, it is a cold <u>7 degrees</u> all year, as water release comes from deep within the reservoir. In addition, the rapids are getting bigger, as the river is too weak to move the boulders washed out of the canyons downstream. As a result of both these problems, some species of <u>fish</u> have become extinct.

Visitors are proving to be powerful allies of the park. Those who once thought that the Grand Canyon was just an awesome hole in the ground soon learn that however big it is, its popularity is in danger of destroying the very qualities that made it one of the <u>seven natural wonders</u> in the world.

Vocabulary

3   Ask students to explain/draw the meaning of the water words: dam, floods, rapids, reservoir and river. You may also want to teach them *drought* – a period of no rain.

Answers
dam – a man-made barrier on a river which forms a lake behind it – usually to provide hydroelectric energy or conserve water
floods – a large amount of water covering land which is normally dry
rapids – the place in a river where there are a lot of large stones and therefore the water flows much faster
reservoir – a man-made lake which is built to provide a source of water for a town or city
river – a large natural stream of water emptying into an ocean, lake or another river.

   In pairs, students should write out sentences that show the difference between the words in each pair.

Answers
A pond is much smaller than a lake.
A stream is much smaller than a river.
A canal is artificial (man-made), whereas a river is natural.
A waterfall is where a river flows over very high rocks and drops to a lower level, whereas rapids are where a river flows between small to medium-sized rocks in the river itself, and so the flow of water is much faster there.

4   Following this exercise is some exam practice in word formation. Students need to make another word from the word in capitals so that the text makes sense. Encourage them to read through the whole text first. They *must* spell the words correctly.

Answers

adjective	noun	adverb	verb
long	length	lengthily	lengthen
weak	weakness	weakly	weaken
deep	depth	deeply	deepen
strong	strength	strongly	strengthen
wide	width	widely	widen
short	shortness	shortly	shorten
warm	warmth	warmly	warm

5

Answers
1 chemical   2 surroundings   3 unwanted
4 poisonous   5 scientists   6 reduction(s)
7 electricity   8 economical NOT economic

Speaking

6   Students should discuss questions a–g in groups.

7   **2 09** Put students in pairs and ask them to read the numbers, letters and words in this exercise aloud. They should note the pronunciation of 'o'.

   Play the recording so they can check their pronunciation.

Recording script
Measurement
thirteen kilometres
thirty centimetres
nought point five kilometres
two point five metres
a hundred and fifty-three kilos
one metre, fifty-three centimetres
a half
a quarter
two thirds
Dates
the first of May, eighteen ninety-nine
the third of August, two thousand
the twelfth of February, two thousand and four
the sixth of September, twenty sixteen
the twenty-fifth of December, nineteen ninety
the fifteenth century
the fourth of the fifth, eleven

Money

ten p or ten pence
one pound forty-five
fifty dollars
twenty euros, thirty cents

'0'

oh one two, three two three, double six, double seven,
eight
three nil
forty love
zero or nought degrees Celsius

Telephone numbers

oh one two five six, three double one, three double nine
oh oh four four, three two four, double six seven oh one
two

Maths

two plus six equals eight
three minus two equals one
four times four equals sixteen
ten divided by two equals five
twenty per cent
three degrees
the square root of sixteen

8 In pairs, students ask and answer questions a–k.

(E)xtension activity

This can be expanded into a team game between students. Ask
them to think up some more questions which require a number
as an answer. For example: maths questions, questions about
historical 'firsts', dates, etc.

15.2 SB pages 100–101

Lesson plan	
Grammar	40–50 minutes
Vocabulary	20–30 minutes
SV	Set 5, which summarises the grammar in this unit, for homework.
LV	See Extension activity for 1.

Countable and uncountable nouns

1 Students make many mistakes with countable and
uncountable nouns. It is something that needs to be
constantly worked at. The columns contain a mixture
of countable and uncountable nouns. Students need to
decide which word in each pair is countable.

Answers

Countable: note, meal, recommendation, journey, job, coin,
storm, verb, vehicle, seat, hairstyle, suitcase, mountain.

These words can be both countable [C] and uncountable [U]:
work [U] the activities you do as part of your job, e.g. *I've got
a lot of work to get through today.* [C] a painting, book, piece
of music, e.g. *the works of Shakespeare*
travel [U] going from one place to another, e.g. *I've always
loved travel.* [C] journeys of exploration, e.g. *We learnt about
the travels of Marco Polo.*
temperature [C] *We had temperatures of minus 20 degrees
last winter.* [U] *There was a sudden rise in temperature
yesterday.*
hair [U] *She has long, curly hair.* [C] an individual hair on the
body or head, e.g. *There was a blond hair on her jacket.*
land [U] area of ground, e.g. *The land was rich and fertile.* [C]
a country, *e.g. the tribal lands of the Maori people*
country [C] an area of land that has its own government, e.g.
Brazil is the largest country in Latin America. [U] land which is
not in towns and is used for farming or left in a natural state,
e.g. *I'd rather live in the country than in a city.*

Draw students' attention to the Corpus spot and ask
them to make a note of the words.

(E)xtension activity

Ask students to explain the use of the following with the
differences in meaning:
paper / a paper – paper you write on and a newspaper
coffee / a coffee – coffee the product and a cup of coffee
experience / an experience – how much time you have spent
doing something and one thing that happened to you
damage / damages – damage to an object and the money you
receive in compensation.

2 Students should look at the information about
determiners before they do this exercise.

Answers

a How **many** of the tourists actually **realise** the problems
they cause?
b Little of the **soil** can be used for cultivation now the trees
have been cut down.
c A large **amount** of equipment **is** needed to camp at the
bottom of the Canyon.
d Only **a small amount of luggage** can be carried on the
back of a donkey down the dirt tracks.
e A large amount of rainforest **is** being cut down every
year.
f The amount of traffic **is** causing too **much congestion** in
major cities.
g **Many** governments **believe** that nuclear power **is** the key
to future energy problems.
h The Park Ranger gave me **a lot of / a great deal of** good
advice about camping in the national park.
i **Few** people nowadays wear fur coats.

3 *A few* and *few* are both used with countable nouns and mean 'a small number of', but *few* on its own is used to emphasise how small that number is. *A little* and *little* are both used with uncountable nouns and mean 'a small amount of', but *little* on its own is used to emphasise how small that amount is.

Answers
few mistakes – not many mistakes = I'm good at English.
a few mistakes – a number of mistakes = I'm quite good at English, but I still make mistakes.
little time – I'm really too busy.
a little time – I do have some time, but it's not very much.

Vocabulary

4 Students need to know the correct expression for limiting an uncountable noun. They can use *a piece of* or *a bit of* but these words are not precise enough.

Answers

a shower of rain	a pane of glass
a slice of cake	a ball of string
an item of clothing	a flash of lightning
a glass of water	a crowd of people
a clap of thunder	a bar of chocolate

5 This exercise summarises the grammar work done in this unit. It can be set for homework if time is short.

Answers
a some; bars
b any/some; flashes
c Some / A few / Many / Most / Lots; panes
d hair
e some advice/information
f any coins
g bag/suitcase; luggage

6

Answers
1 few
2 ago
3 in
4 deal/amount
5 Although/Though
6 of
7 which/that
8 one

Exam folder 8

SB pages 102–103

Paper 3 Part 4 Multiple choice

Let students read through the introduction and Advice.

1 **2 10** Check that the students know what an ecolodge is. They could brainstorm what they think might be found there – recycling, natural materials, fairtrade food/coffee, solar power, etc.

Ask the students to look at options A, B and C for question 1, then listen to the recording as far as 'travelling by myself for the first time'.

2 Ask the students to decide on the correct answer, which is C. A is wrong because she had enjoyed the journey and was excited. B is wrong because she wasn't worried about changing planes.

3 **2 11** Ask the students to read through questions 2–7 and try to predict what they might hear. Now, play the recording, which is heard twice.

Answers
1 C   2 B   3 A   4 C   5 B   6 A   7 B

Recording script

You will hear a radio interview with a girl called Lisa Greene, who is talking about her stay at an ecolodge, an environmentally friendly hotel in Costa Rica, Central America. For questions 1–7, choose the best answer (A, B or C).

Interviewer: I'd like to welcome Lisa Greene to the studio today. Lisa, you won a competition in a magazine to stay at an ecolodge, an environmentally friendly hotel in Costa Rica, didn't you?

Lisa: That's right. I had to write an article about recycling and why it is a good thing for the planet.

Interviewer: You hadn't travelled outside of Europe before – how did you feel about the journey?

Lisa: Well, I flew to Costa Rica from London and then had to take a small plane to an airport very near the ecolodge. I was then picked up at the local airport by the ecolodge manager in an electric car. It all took a bit longer than I was expecting but then I was only used to short journeys within Europe. Anyway, I was so excited I didn't care about having to change planes or travelling by myself for the first time.

Interviewer: I'm told the site of the ecolodge is amazing. You must have seen quite a few animals and birds?

Lisa: Yes. It's high up on a mountainside with incredible views of the surrounding forest and the sea. It has an observation gallery, where you can sit and look over the rainforest. I particularly liked it when the parrots, which were amazingly gentle and unafraid, came and sat by me, hoping for a piece of fruit. There were also monkeys in the forest but they were too shy to come up close. People are often disappointed that I didn't see any large animals like jaguars – but these are actually quite rare now.

Interviewer: What was your accommodation like?

Lisa: There were 16 small, really nice bungalows built around the central building. As it's environmentally friendly, there's no air conditioning, but the bungalows each have a roof which shades the outside of the building. Another good idea, especially for me, is that if you leave a light on accidentally, it will automatically switch itself off after 20 minutes. I also really liked the outdoor shower but was really puzzled at first when I got back all hot and sweaty to find there was only cold water to wash in. This was because all the water is heated by solar power and when the hot water is finished you just have to wait for the sun to heat up some more!

Interviewer: So what did you do while you were there? Did you go for walks through the forest?

Lisa: Yes. You can hike through the forest with one of the local guides or you can choose from 13 different well-marked trails and go by yourself. Each one takes all day and you do need to be in good shape as the paths aren't always very easy. It's really worth it though, just to hear the noise the birds make and to catch glimpses of them flying through the trees.

Interviewer: What about swimming – did you manage to do that?

Lisa: I went to the beach a few times as it's only a thirty-minute walk away. It's a beautiful sandy beach, and the sea and beach are absolutely clean – no litter or anything to ruin it. Another day I went swimming in a natural pool under a waterfall. It was a real highlight of my trip. The water was really cold and refreshing. As you can imagine, I didn't miss the fact that there wasn't a swimming pool at the place I was staying.

Interviewer: Now one reason for your trip was to see the conservation centre in action, wasn't it?

Lisa: Yes. The centre supplies the ecolodge with organic food but this is just a minor part of what they do. What the centre was built for is to develop green construction techniques using local materials and teach young people in the area how to use them. The people there were really friendly and I learnt a lot about their area. It's not really set up for tourists, so I was very lucky to be invited to visit.

Interviewer: It must have been sad to leave. Are you going to write up your experience for the magazine?

Lisa: Yes, I have to send the magazine another article – this time on my trip. It needs to be at the magazine by the end of November so it can be in the January edition. I know it'll be online from February, if you want to read it and can't afford to buy a copy.

Interviewer: Thank you, Lisa. And next week …

16 Eat to live

Topic Food

16.1

Listening	Talking about food
Exam skills	Reading and Use of English Paper 1 Part 6
	Speaking Paper 4 Part 3
Vocabulary	Collocations – food

16.2

Grammar focus	The article
	Possession
	Expressions of time

Workbook contents

Reading and Use of English Paper 1 Part 7 – multiple matching
Listening Paper 3 Part 3 – multiple matching
Grammar – the article
Reading and Use of English Paper 1 Part 2 – open cloze

16.1 SB pages 104–105

Lesson plan

Listening	10–15 minutes
Reading	30–40 minutes
Vocabulary	5–10 minutes
Speaking	10–15 minutes

SV   Set 7 for homework; omit 1 and/or 8.
LV   See Extension activities after 3 and 7.

Listening

1   Ask students to make a list of what they normally eat in a day and then discuss what they've written with a partner. This exercise could be quite sensitive if there are students in the class who are overweight or underweight. It can be easily omitted.

2   Ask students to speculate on what people in Japan, Alaska and California eat. If the students are Japanese, then they could say what the stereotype of what they eat is and say whether it is true or not.

Background information
The Inuit is the proper name for what used to be called the Eskimo people who live within the Arctic Circle.

3   **2 12** On the recording are three women talking about what they normally eat. Students should take notes of what is said. Play the recording as often as needed. Round up this exercise by asking students which diet they would prefer and why.

Answers
Akiko
Breakfast	soup, rice, fish
Lunch	noodles, hamburgers
Dinner	pasta, soup
Also eats vegetables.

Kunu
Breakfast	cheese sandwich, orange juice
Lunch	raw fish
Supper	reindeer, fish
Hardly ever eats sweet food.

Gayle
Breakfast	omelette
Lunch	sandwich – tuna, tomato paste, non-fat bread
Dinner	grilled fish, chicken
Does not eat fat.

Extension activity

To give students more practice in note taking, you could do a jigsaw listening. Divide the class into three groups (A, B and C) and get them to take extensive notes about one person (not just about what they eat). Rearrange the groups into a mixed group with an A, a B and a C member and ask them to discuss what they found out.

Recording script
Speaker 1: My name is Akiko and I was born in Hiroshima in Japan. I moved to England with my family when I was three but my mother always makes us traditional Japanese food. For breakfast we have soup, rice and fish. For lunch I eat noodles, but I also love hamburgers. It's very common for Japanese people to mix traditional and Western food. I'm conscious of healthy eating and I eat a lot of vegetables, but I don't worry about my weight! In the evening I'll have pasta or some more soup.
Speaker 2: My name is Kunu, and I grew up in Alaska, where meals are central to Inuit life. I moved to Seattle when I was seventeen, and became physically ill because my body rejected Western foods. I do eat some Western food though. For breakfast I always have a cheese sandwich with orange juice. Lunch is

82   UNIT 16

usually raw fish, and for supper I have reindeer or fish. I hardly eat any sweet foods and I exercise five times a week.

Speaker 3: Everyone calls me Gayle. I exercise for about half an hour before breakfast, which is usually an omelette. For lunch I'll have a sandwich – a mixture of tuna and tomato paste on non-fat bread. I eat a lot but I never eat fat. If I go out to eat, I always ask the waiter to miss out the cream or cheese or oil. People are used to it in LA. I keep a journal every day to say what exercise I've done and exactly what I've eaten. In the evening I'll have grilled fish or chicken.

4 **Thinking about the answers to the questions should help students with the text they are going to read.**

> **Suggested answers**
> - Yes, it's ripe and probably juicy.
> - No, it's not ripe.
> - No, it's probably stale. / I prefer crunchy biscuits.
> - No, it's mouldy.
> - No, it will taste awful. / I prefer sparkling lemonade.
> - No, it will probably be raw.

Reading

5 **Students should skim the text, that is, read it very quickly to get an idea of what it is about. They shouldn't worry too much about vocabulary. They should then look at sentences A–G and decide which one should go in gaps 1–6.**

> **Answers**
> 1 F   2 A   3 D   4 E   5 C   6 G

6 **These questions follow on from the topic of the text. Ask students to discuss them in groups.**

Vocabulary

7 **This exercise can be set for homework if time is short.**

> **Answers**
> a rich   b off
> c tough   d ripe
> e mild   f rotten
> g weak   h bad

Extension activity

In the article there was the expression *in fact*. Here are some more expressions with *in*. Ask students to match the expression on the left with the explanation on the right. Then ask them to write sentences using the expressions. If they are uncertain, tell them to use their dictionaries and remind them that, as well as giving the meaning of words, dictionaries can also help them to understand how words and expressions are used.

in fact	owing money
in common	actually
in debt	using a pen
in the end	crying
in particular	finally
in public	divided in two
in ink	shared
in tears	used to give an alternative explanation of something
in other words	especially
in half	in places where people can see you

> **Answers**
> in fact – actually
> in common – shared
> in debt – owing money
> in the end – finally
> in particular – especially
> in public – in places where people can see you
> in ink – using a pen
> in tears – crying
> in other words – used to give an alternative explanation of something
> in half – divided in two

Speaking

8 **This exercise gives practice in Part 3 of the Speaking paper. Explain the situation to the students and ask them to decide which two ideas they would favour. The students then form a different pair and discuss their previous choices and defend them, if necessary.**

16.2 SB pages 106–107

Lesson plan	
Grammar	60–90 minutes
SV	Set 4 for homework.
LV	See Extension activity after 5.

The article

1 **The aim of this part of Unit 16 is to look at nouns. This first exercise revises and extends the work done on countable and uncountable nouns in Unit 15.**

2

3 The gaps in the article can have more than one answer. Check students understand the possible differences.

4 Using an article or not can change the meaning of some English expressions. For example:

I went to the hospital to see a sick friend.

I went to hospital because I was sick.

They go to church every Sunday.

We visited the church to look for my great-aunt's grave.

Her brother is in prison for burglary.

Our drama group sometimes puts on plays in the prison.

Also you *play football*, but *play the violin*.

Possession

5 Students are often confused about how to indicate possession in English. They have a tendency to only use *of*.

Ask students to read through the information about possession. This is a simplified list of rules about possession, suitable for intermediate students. They should then read the sentences and correct them, if necessary, giving reasons for their choice of answer.

Corpus spot

Ask the students to correct the sentences. Some sentences contain unnecessary articles or prepositions and others require students to add an article.

Extension activity

Ask students to bring in their favourite recipe and tell their partner how to make it. Give help with vocabulary (*chop, fry, boil, bake, stir, mix, add*, etc.) before they start and remind them to use the imperative when giving instructions.

Writing folder 8

SB pages 108–109

Paper 2 Part 1 Essays

1 Ask students to read the exam question and underline informal language in the answer.

Sample answer

Informal language is underlined.

This essay discusses the advantages and disadvantages of cycling to work in an urban environment. It considers traffic congestion, the dangers to cyclists and the savings that can be made by using two wheels instead of four.

Nowadays there are <u>loads of cars</u> and trucks on the roads, causing long queues of traffic, especially during the rush hour. For drivers, the stress of waiting in a traffic jam must be <u>unbelievable</u>. <u>So why don't they</u> leave their vehicles at home and cycle instead?

<u>Well, perhaps</u>. Some people argue that it is healthier but <u>I don't agree! You end up</u> breathing in car fumes and risking your life every single day – cycling in cities can be incredibly dangerous and you can get seriously hurt.

On the other hand, it is much cheaper to use a bike. You don't have to buy petrol or pay for many repairs. <u>I guess</u> for this reason it is preferable to cycle to work, but only if you can avoid the busy main roads and follow more pleasant routes.

In conclusion, <u>yes</u>, we should cycle wherever possible. However, not enough is being done to encourage people to leave their cars at home and this needs to be addressed urgently.

2 Ask students to discuss how they could reword the underlined words and phrases, making any changes necessary.

Possible rewording

loads of – substantial numbers of

unbelievable – considerable

So why don't they – Therefore, isn't it more sensible for them to

Well, perhaps – The answer to this is not straightforward.

I don't agree! – This isn't necessarily the case.

You end up – As a cyclist, you have to breathe in … and risk

I guess – (omit)

yes – it is certainly true that

3

Suggested answers

Possible solutions: **a, c, e, f, h**

a The key to reducing the number of cars on the road is to impose higher taxes on motorists.

c It is essential to restrict the opportunities for parking in the city centre.

e One of the biggest challenges in the short term will be how to persuade people to take public transport but with lower speed limits for private cars, that might become a more attractive option.

f The key to reducing traffic is to raise petrol prices substantially, so that driving becomes the less obvious choice.

h It is vital that the number of cars in a city is restricted, so issuing driving permits for use on certain days seems a good policy to adopt.

4 Ask students to reorder the sentences and elicit answers.

Answers

a What is of high priority is the introduction of tighter laws on older vehicles, whose exhaust fumes cause greater pollution.

b In the short term, it is essential to consult the public, whose concerns have never been fully aired.

c Instant action is needed to reduce the volume of cars in our cities, while in the medium term, further research should be carried out on alternative forms of transport.

5 Ask students to make a paragraph plan and check their ideas.

6 Set the essay for homework.

Sample answer

TRAFFIC IN OUR CITIES

The volume of traffic in most cities has reached an unsustainable level and urgent action is needed. This essay considers the importance of public transport and suggests other ways of restricting the use of private cars.

Any city needs to have an efficient and reliable public transport network . This requires regular investment, but funding is not always available. In addition, as fares are so high, it can be more cost-effective for people to drive themselves.

It is clearly vital to find ways of reducing the numbers of cars on the road. The key to this may be to impose higher taxes on motorists, or to restrict parking in cities. Furthermore, if petrol prices were raised substantially, driving would become the less obvious choice.

Finally, people should be persuaded to think twice before making an unnecessary journey. More companies are supporting staff wishing to work from home rather than commuting, and with online shopping, fewer trips to the supermarket should be necessary.

In conclusion, improvements to public transport are only part of the solution to reducing traffic. As a society, we need to look at other ways of minimising the use of private cars, including lifestyle changes.

(197 words)

17.1

Exam skills	Speaking Paper 4 Part 2
	Listening Paper 3 Part 1
Vocabulary	Phrasal verbs and expressions with *look*

17.2

Grammar focus	Relative clauses
	Relative pronouns: *who, whom, whose*
Vocabulary	Word formation
Exam skills	Reading and Use of English Paper 1 Part 2

Workbook contents

Reading and Use of English Paper 1 Part 3 – word formation
Vocabulary – *like*
Writing – relative clauses
Reading and Use of English Paper 1 Part 2 – open cloze

17.1 SB pages 110–111

Lesson plan

Speaking	30–40 minutes
Listening	20–30 minutes
Vocabulary	15–20 minutes

SV Omit 3 and 5.
LV See Extension activity after 5; elicit more answers in 6.

Speaking

1   In this unit, the long turn (Paper 4 Part 2) is practised in full. Refer students to the Exam spot and, if necessary, to the information about the Speaking test on page 7.

Explain that it is better for a candidate to keep talking for the full minute, rather than 'dry up'.

Ask students to read their instructions and allow them a minute or so to think about the notes for Student A, which are there to help them on the first long turn. (The football pins and badges are worn on the waistcoat of an Aston Villa – a Birmingham football team – fan.)

Start them talking and keep an eye on the time yourself. Stop the A students after one minute. Then ask Student B to make a brief comment as instructed.

Have a brief class discussion before starting the next long turn with the second pair of photos. Check that the Student As did compare the two photos. Elicit the type of comments made by the Student Bs. Refer them to the useful language for giving opinions in Unit 6 if necessary (page 41).

2   The pictures show a woman with her collection of hub caps and a woman whose hobby is making jewellery. As students do the task, walk round and listen to some of the pairs. Do not interrupt or correct them, but make a mental note of any feedback you can give later.

After the minute is up, Student A should make a brief comment as indicated. Then elicit the ideas that came up in the pairs, listing the main ones on the board. Show students that there is in fact a lot that can be said about a pair of photos.

3   Set a time limit of three minutes for the team activity. Check which team has the longer list and write some of the hobbies on the board under the two headings: *Collectors* and *Creators*. Then ask students to decide on the four most interesting from these lists. Elicit opinions from the class afterwards.

Listening

4   **2 13** Explain that students are now going to hear a complete set of listening short extracts and do the eight multiple-choice questions as in Paper 3 Part 1. Refer them back to Exam folder 6 (pages 76–77) if necessary before they start. Then play the recording straight through. Each extract is repeated.

Go through the answers and deal with any problems, quoting from the recording script or replaying the extracts concerned. The photograph at the bottom of the page shows slot-car racing (question 8).

Answers
1 B   2 C   3 B   4 A   5 A   6 A   7 B   8 C

Recording script

You will hear people talking in eight different situations. For questions 1-8, choose the best answer (A, B or C).

1   You hear a woman talking about making jewellery.

Woman: 2003 was the year my passion for jewellery making began – there was a fantastic art teacher at school who made earrings and bracelets out of copper, and I thought, I want to do that one day too! I found an evening class, where I learned a lot of useful techniques for working with gold and silver. I've never considered using the former for my own jewellery because it's outside my price range, but I can afford the latter and in fact I've made several things with it recently.

2 You hear two friends talking about postcards.

Man: Here are those cards I bought for you in Oxford, to add to your collection. I hope you don't think they're too tatty – they must be at least fifty years old.

Woman: Thanks. The condition they're in doesn't bother me. And actually, looking at the stamps, they're older than you say, which is brilliant because I haven't got many from the 1930s.

Man: Oh, so you're looking for cards from a certain period?

Woman: Well, I collect all sorts, but I'm on the lookout for older ones that have text on the picture. Like this one, which says: 'Thinking of you in St Ives'.

3 You hear a radio talk about wooden objects.

Woman: I knew someone once who had an absolute passion for making things out of wood. He spent hours and hours on his hobby – whatever the object was, he always took great pride in doing it well and making it unique, by choosing a special wood. He never chose the same kind twice. He would make all sorts of things – a new handle for a fork, with a pattern cut into it; enough models to fill several glass cases ... He even made an electric guitar, which he painted designs on – something he didn't normally do. One piece I remember well is a polar bear. The way it was carved really captured the look of the animal, walking heavily through the snow.

4 You hear a man talking about his hobby.

Man: People think it's a bit odd that I spend my weekends dressed up in anything from metal armour to old uniforms, out in the open air. But it's good fun! The group that puts on these events was only formed about four months ago. I joined in April and we've already performed five battles! You learn a great deal about history, because everything is researched properly – from the costumes to the actual battle tactics. My girlfriend's not too pleased with me at the moment. I'm going to have to miss her birthday 'cos we're doing the Battle of Naseby. That's not the reason she's mad at me though. She wanted to come too but I wouldn't let her!

5 You hear a girl talking about collecting beads.

Interviewer: This is Radio QB, the phone lines are open and we want to hear about *your* hobbies. And here's Eleanor, from London. What are you into, Eleanor?

Eleanor: Beads. I've got several hundred, in all shapes and sizes – glass, metal, plastic ones ... They're from all over the world, too: I've got a handful of beautiful wooden ones from India and some very unusual African ones carved out of bone. A few of them I've made up into earrings and necklaces, but what I really like doing is collecting! Especially coloured glass ones, which I've got loads of.

Interviewer: And you say you've got several hundred – how long has it taken you to get so many?

Eleanor: Not that long, really ... I had lots of plastic ones when I was a kid, but I gave those away, so they don't count! I suppose I got serious about beads three years ago. Since then, my family have given me tins of beads as presents, and I spend most of my pocket money on them too.

6 You hear part of a conversation in a radio play.

Man: Well, I've rung them twice already and they said I must take the matter up with you. It's clearly your responsibility as I got the model kit from you in the first place. It was sealed when I got it too. No, I'm quite sure. I buy a lot of your kits, you know. Do you want me to contact Model Makers magazine and tell them about what's happened? You have all my details, so I suggest you sort it out!

7 You hear an interview with a girl who collects pebbles.

Interviewer: I'm with Jenny Braintree, who paints the whole world in miniature on small stones she finds at the seaside. Jenny, you took up this hobby four years ago ...

Jenny: Er ... it was four months ago, in fact. I was on a beach holiday with my parents and I collected loads of nice smooth pebbles. When I got home, I started to paint tiny images of beautiful places like the Swiss mountains and the Brazilian rainforest. I've done 89 so far.

Interviewer: Amazing! These pictures are no more than five centimetres across and yet they contain so much detail! So what's the reason behind this, Jenny? Do you earn anything from all your hard work?

Jenny: Dad thinks I could sell them but I'm not interested in that and anyway they're too special to me. My real aim is to get better at painting because that's what I want to do when I'm older. And although I haven't been to the places I illustrate on the pebbles, it can be really good fun finding out about them on the internet.

8 You hear an interview with a boy whose hobby is slot-car racing.

Interviewer: Jamie Eagle, who is the outright winner of today's slot-car racing, is with me now.

Congratulations, Jamie, and this is now your tenth win! So where did it all begin? I know your father was also racing here today. Did he know what he was doing when he persuaded you to take up such a time-consuming hobby?

Jamie: Erm, actually, it was *me* who persuaded *him* – he's only been racing this year. He's pretty hopeless at it, too! No, it was my cousin who's to blame. He used to take me along when he went to race meetings – I was five at the time – and I thought it was just brilliant!

Interviewer: And if your father's racing his own car, who do you have as back-up today?

Jamie: I've introduced my friend Ian to slot-car racing – at the moment he's free to help me, though next year he hopes to have a car of his own.

5 Encourage students to give reasons for their choice of hobbies that would interest them least.

Extension activity

Include some vocabulary work on negative adjectives before this discussion. Put these adjectives up on the board and ask students to organise them in four meaning groups.

tedious	time-consuming	dull	expensive
boring	fiddly	overpriced	tricky
costly	trivial	unimportant	silly

Answers
expensive, overpriced, costly
tedious, dull, boring
silly, trivial, unimportant
time-consuming, tricky, fiddly

Vocabulary

6 Check students understand the phrases and phrasal verbs in a–j before they go through questions 1–10. Encourage students to use their imagination to the full. Elicit at least one answer from everyone in the class.

Suggested answers
1 A a doctor   B a plumber   C a mechanic
2 A sew   B cook   C translate
3 A a coastguard   B a detective / the police
 C an accountant / a business person
4 A shiny and expensive   B dark brown
 C dull and grey
5 A a doctor   B a gardener   C an MP / the city council
6 A ... these bank charges are completely unreasonable!
 B ... you can't stay up to watch that programme on TV.
 C ... my private life is my own concern.

7 A the reason(s) why the proposal was turned down
 B fresh facts about the crime
 C practical information such as visa requirements and likely living costs
8 A someone was crossing the road
 B a big wave was about to hit you
 C a pot of paint was in danger of toppling over
9 A his older brother or sister   B a professor
 C the head chef
10 A reaching the finish   B seeing his/her family
 C going away for a long weekend

17.2 SB pages 112–113

Lesson plan	
Grammar	40–50 minutes
Vocabulary	30–40 minutes

SV   Set 5 and 10 for homework.
LV   See Extension activity after 4.

Relative clauses

1 Students discuss examples **a** and **b** in pairs. Check understanding before referring them to the Grammar folder, page 173. Then elicit the difference in meaning between **c** and **d**.

Answers
a Only some of the children were tired, so not all of them went to bed. (defining relative clause)
b All the children were tired and all went to bed. (non-defining relative clause)
c They wanted a hotel with a pool, so they probably passed several which didn't have pools before they came to one which did. (defining relative clause)
d They stayed at the very first hotel they came to and, fortunately, it had a pool. (non-defining relative clause)

2

Answers
a has a non-defining relative clause
b has a defining relative clause   c which N
d who D   e who D   f whose N
g (most of) which N   h that D

3 Elicit the missing pronoun and refer students to the Grammar folder, page 173 if necessary. Students can work through a–e in pairs.

Answers
Here are those cards **which/that** I bought for you in Oxford.

a that/which I wanted to buy
b who/that I really looked up to
c that/which I can't stand about Harry
d who/that you met at John's party
e that/which we stayed at

4 Ask students to read the explanation and then work through examples a–d.

> **Answers**
> **a** where **b** when **c** who **d** which

Extension activity

Ask students to write five sentences containing *where*, *when* and *why* clauses on a piece of paper, one under the other. These should be a mixture of defining and non-defining relative clauses. They should fold the paper over so that only the bottom sentence is visible. Then ask them to get into groups of four or five and pass their sheet to the person on their right. Each person should tick the sentence if they think the *wh-* word can be omitted. If they are right, they stay in the game. If not, they sit back and advise the others. The winner is the person who continues to give the right answer for the most turns.

Relative pronouns

5

> **Answers**
> **a** from whom I have bought …
> **b** for whom my sister worked …
> **c** with whom I went riding, …

6

> **Answers**
> **a** The singer, whose art collection is now worth millions, has always been a fan …
> **b** Maria, whose hobbies include skydiving and collecting antiques, works in a bank …
> **c** The hot air balloon, whose first flight was made in 1783, was designed by the …
> **d** Collectors, whose number has doubled over the last decade, form an increasingly large part of the buyers at local auctions.

Vocabulary

7

> **Answers**
> **a** delight **b** elegance **c** exception **d** mass
> **e** remark **f** substance

8

> **Answers**
> *emphasising attractiveness*   delightful, elegant
> *emphasising extent*   massive, substantial
> *emphasising rarity*   exceptional, remarkable

9

> **Answers**
> **1** more **2** which/that
> **3** whose **4** as
> **5** from **6** ought
> **7** not **8** would

10

> **Possible collocations**
> a delightful painting   an elegant woman
> an exceptional challenge   on a massive scale
> a remarkable memory   a substantial amount

Exam folder 9

SB pages 114–115

Paper 1 Part 6 Gapped text

Refer students to the advice given before they do the task.

> **Answers**
> **1** B **2** G **3** D **4** A **5** C **6** E

18.1

Exam skills	Reading and Use of English Paper 1 Part 5
Vocabulary	Phrasal verbs with *come* and *go*

18.2

Listening	Matching books to speakers
Grammar focus	*enough, too, very, so, such*
Exam skills	Reading and Use of English Paper 1 Parts 2 and 4

Workbook contents

Reading and Use of English Paper 1 Part 6 – gapped text
Vocabulary – books and writing
Grammar – *so, such, too, very, enough*
Listening Paper 3 Part 4 – multiple choice

18.1 SB pages 116–117

Lesson plan

Reading	45–60 minutes
Vocabulary	20–30 minutes

SV   Keep 1 and 2 brief.
LV   See Extension activities for 4 and 5.

Reading

1   The illustration shows two people fishing from a small boat in a quiet lagoon. The book is mainly set in a group of tiny islands known as the Sundarbans, which lie in the Bay of Bengal. The word 'Sundarban' can be translated from Bengali as 'beautiful forest' and the Sundarbans are a UNESCO world heritage site, with the largest area of tidal mangrove forest in the world.

Background information
Amitav Ghosh is an Indian writer, born July 11, 1956 in Kolkata (Calcutta). *The Hungry Tide* was published in 2005. His next book, *Sea of Poppies*, was shortlisted for the 2008 Man Booker Prize. Amitav Ghosh has also written non-fiction books and essays.

2   Give students time to read the reviews and elicit their ideas.

Possible answers
The first review talks about adventure, so the novel could have an exciting plot. It also refers to personal identity and there's a love story, it seems, as well as some historical references.

The second review praises the author for being able to develop a plot from very little – so the book might be about ordinary people, I suppose?

3   **Ask students to skim the first paragraph. Encourage them to work out the meaning of any words they don't know from the surrounding context. Give them a couple of minutes to read the first paragraph and then elicit answers.**

Answer
The action in this extract takes place on a train that has recently left Kolkata (Calcutta) in India.

The main character, a young woman called Piya, is mentioned in the second line of the opening paragraph and it is clear that she is travelling with a lot of luggage (she has more than one backpack).

Students are unlikely to know the word *arrayed* but can probably picture the scene, with Piya's luggage spread out around her.

4   **Ask students to work in pairs. Give them enough time to discuss the questions and then elicit their answers. If necessary, explain why the other options are wrong (see detailed explanation below).**

Answers
1 D   2 C   3 A   4 B   5 C   6 B

Detailed explanation:
1   Multiple-choice questions at this B2 level will often require some inference, as here. The answer (**D**) comes from two places in the first paragraph: *an unexpected stroke of luck presented Piya with an opportunity to go for a seat beside a window* and *she had been sitting in the stuffiest part of the train compartment, on the edge of a bench*. **A** is wrong because she was already sitting down. **B** is not suggested in the text beyond the distraction of *the train had stopped at a station called Champahati*. **C**, although plausible, is not stated, so we don't know whether there is more room for her backpacks or not.
2   The answer (**C**) comes from *somehow, in the ten days she had spent in India she had developed an unexpected taste for milky, overboiled tea* and *there were no spices in it for one thing, and this was more to her taste than the chai back home*. **A** is wrong because the chai is different from what she drinks in Seattle. **B** is wrong because although the Indian chai mentioned has no spices in it and could therefore be described as 'bland', Piya is not 'disappointed' by this fact, as she finds it more to her taste. **D** is not suggested by the text.

3 The answer (**A**) comes towards the end of the fourth paragraph, in the words *she had been struck by the self-satisfied tilt of his head and the way in which he stared at everyone around him …* **B** is wrong as he didn't know any of the people he was looking at, but was *taking them in, sizing them up, sorting them all into their places.* **C** is not suggested by the text and **D** does not reflect Piya's initial reaction when she had first seen the man on the platform. It is important to read each question carefully, not just the options.

4 This question requires some reading between the lines of the text to work out Piya's thoughts and behaviour. The answer (**B**) comes from text immediately before the quoted *But how did you guess? – Piya had no wish to get into an argument so she let this pass. Instead she opened her eyes wide and, in an attempt to restore peace…* and her strategy is also confirmed by the later statement *This seemed to do the trick.* **A** and **C** are plausible but not true to the text. **D** is wrong as the man had already acknowledged her apology.

5 The answer (**C**) is confirmed by Piya's implication that she knows what is ahead of her *I'll do what I usually do … in my line of work there's not much talk needed.* **B** and **D** are ruled out because of this (she doesn't need to communicate much to do her job, either in English or in the local languages). And **A** is wrong because she is relaxed and confident about the work.

6 The answer (**B**) comes from the adverb *sharply* and the fact that he interrupts her to say that he knows what the term means. **A** is wrong because although he understands the basic meaning of 'cetologist', the text doesn't suggest that he knows 'quite a bit' about it. **C** and **D** are plausible but not stated in this extract.

Vocabulary

5 These are examples of two- and three-part phrasal verbs, the meanings of which are given below.

> **Answers**
> *go for* – try to get
> *come out with* – say something suddenly and unexpectedly
>
> **a** come up with **b** go ahead **c** went up **d** went by
> **e** came out **f** came across **g** went through **h** gone off

Extension activity

Ask students to look at the particles *across, ahead, by*, etc. again and brainstorm other phrasal verbs they know that use them, for example: *keep up with, meet up, get through, fall out, keep off, get by, look ahead, get across.*

18.2 SB 118–119

Lesson plan	
Listening	15–20 minutes
Grammar	55–70 minutes

SV   Set 5 or 6 for homework.
LV   See Extension activity for 2.

Listening

1 Ask students to identify the books. Remind them to look at the covers and think about the titles.

> **Answers**
> **A** play **B** biography **C** science fiction
> **D** historical novel **E** non-fiction **F** crime novel

2 🔊 **14** Play the recording straight through and ask students to decide on their answers. Check answers, playing the recording again if necessary.

> **Answers**
> **1** D **2** E **3** B **4** C **5** F

> **Recording script**
> **Speaker 1:** All of her books are really well researched and they're full of amazing details about what daily life used to be like, so you learn a lot about that period. It's extremely imaginative, the characters are very realistic and, as the title suggests, there's a murder mystery too. This is the seventh one of hers I've read and I can't wait to get my hands on another!
>
> **Speaker 2:** I found the book fascinating, but at the same time it's more than a little depressing. We're so dependent on these creatures! The writers consider the planet's future, suggesting what might happen if they died out completely. It's a really scary possibility actually, because their disappearance would affect the food chain dramatically – in only four years, apparently.
>
> **Speaker 3:** I don't normally read lengthy books of this kind, but I'd enjoyed several of his novels, so I was interested to find out more about the man himself. It's certainly comprehensive and thoroughly researched, but I have to admit I found it a little hard-going in places – the writer's own account of his experiences is so much more colourful. Still, it's worth keeping on the shelves to revisit one day.
>
> **Speaker 4:** A friend lent me the first book written by this author, which I enjoyed, but this one is loads better. It's the same character from the previous story but he's a lot more developed somehow. It's set a few centuries ahead of now, and the vision of how a society so

different to ours might operate is really powerful. I got completely carried along with the storyline, and the dialogue is fantastic too. Yes, a great read!

Speaker 5: Once I started it, I just couldn't put it down. The plot is quite complicated and it moves along at a really fast pace. What I like best about it is the two main characters – they have such different personalities. The private investigator himself is quite jokey and upbeat, while his business partner is a rather mysterious figure. He's an ex-police officer, who says very little but is always there to provide backup when things get tough. This is the ninth title in the series, but I haven't read them all yet.

Extension activity

Include an optional class discussion about everybody's favourite type of book, referring to the categories listed in 1 and using some of the expressions from the extracts.

enough, too, very, so, such

Corpus spot

The *Cambridge Learner Corpus* also shows that students make mistakes in the spelling of *enough*, e.g. 'enought'.

3

> **Answers**
> Yes, the writer does believe the book has a future. Reasons (in second paragraph): people have more leisure time to read in; the book has a strong tradition; it's very practical.
>
> **1** as   **2** would   **3** besides   **4** why   **5** used
> **6** from   **7** not   **8** be

DO YOU WANT TO CHECK STUDENT PROGRESS?
PROGRESS TEST 9 ON THE TEACHER'S RESOURCES CD-ROM

4   Students can do this on their own or in pairs.

> **Answers**
> **a** enough reasons
> **b** small enough
> **c** This is the extra statement – common expressions of this type are: *funnily enough, strangely enough,* etc. For example: *Funnily enough, my friend had bought the same book for me.*
> **d** too dismissive; too much
> **e** and by other technological attractions, too
> **f** very badly injured; very strong pull
> **g** so effective
> **h** the last hundred years or so
> **i** If that is so,
> **j** such alternatives to books as
> **k** such a practical tool

5

> **Answers**
> **a** enough time   **b** large enough
> **c** enough books   **d** had had enough of
> **e** not enough people   **f** got enough to
> **g** quite enough about   **h** Funnily enough

6

> **Answers**
> **1** such cold weather (that) we
> **2** too little time to give
> **3** so well (that) you should/could
> **4** is very good at getting
> **5** takes such a lot of / takes such a long
> **6** (this is) so, a refund

Writing folder 9

SB pages 120–121

Paper 2 Part 2 Reviews

Remind students that film and TV reviews were covered in Writing folder 6.

1   Ask students to find and correct the mistakes. Elicit their answers.

> **Answers**
> *The mistakes are highlighted.*
> The book 'Marcovaldo', by Italo Calvino is one of the jewels of 20th century fiction. It is actually a series of twenty short stories, all focusing on the same caracter – Marcovaldo – who lives with his large family in an unnamed city in the north of italy. Each story is set, in a diferent season: there are five about living in the city in summer, and so on.
>
> Many aspects of modern life are described, such as

advertiseing and pollution of the enviroment, though the book is not completly true to life. This is perhaps it's greatest strength. It has a unique mixture of realistic events and bizzare ones, which often take the reader by surprise.

One particluar story features the publicity campains of rival soap powder manufacturers. Marcovaldos' children and their frends collect hundreds of free cartons of washing powder, which they hope to sell to people in the neibourhood. In the end, they have to get rid of everything quickly and so throw the cartons into the River. The story closes with a memorable descricion of soap bubbles being blown over the city their whiteness competing with the black factory smoke. Black wins.

Corrected version

The book 'Marcovaldo', by Italo Calvino, is one of the jewels of 20th-century fiction. It is actually a series of twenty short stories, all focusing on the same character – Marcovaldo – who lives with his large family in an unnamed city in the north of Italy. Each story is set in a different season: there are five about living in the city in summer, and so on.

Many aspects of modern life are described, such as advertising and pollution of the environment, though the book is not completely true to life. This is perhaps its greatest strength. It has a unique mixture of realistic events and bizarre ones, which often take the reader by surprise.

One particular story features the publicity campaigns of rival soap powder manufacturers. Marcovaldo's children and their friends collect hundreds of free cartons of washing powder, which they hope to sell to people in the neighbourhood. In the end, they have to get rid of everything quickly and so throw the cartons into the river. The story closes with a memorable description of soap bubbles being blown over the city, their whiteness competing with the black factory smoke. Black wins.

2 The most suitable final paragraph is B. (A refers to a novel and C is too negative and so doesn't fit with the rest of the review.)

3 Give students time to sort the nouns into the two categories and elicit answers.

Answers

Characters: ambition, attitude, determination, enthusiasm, loyalty, manner, mood, reputation, sympathy, temper
Events: action, adventure, chaos, impact, incident, mood, theme
Mood and *reputation* can apply to both characters and events.

4 Ask students to complete the sentences, using suitable nouns from 3.

Answers

a loyalty   b sympathy   c chaos   d reputation   e impact
f manner   g theme   h incident

5 Allow students to choose the question they prefer.

Answers

STARTED EARLY, TOOK MY DOG, BY KATE ATKINSON

This wonderful novel is one of a series featuring Jackson Brodie, who is a private investigator. Kate Atkinson has developed Jackson's character across the books and in this particular novel, we feel quite sympathetic towards him, as he has a rather complicated and not totally successful life.

We learn a lot about Jackson from his actual words and the author is brilliant at writing sharp and amusing dialogue. I can recommend the novel to anyone of my age with a sense of humour and I guarantee you will laugh out loud at times.

Another interesting character in the novel is a retired police officer called Tracy Waterhouse, whose life is turned upside down by a chance event and the decision she makes as a result. We get to know Tracy through her inner thoughts on how she sees the world around her. The contrast between Tracy's life and Jackson's is fascinating.

There is a whole cast of other characters to enjoy, not to mention more than one dog, as suggested by the title. Read this book soon!

(185 words)

THE OLD MAN AND THE SEA, BY ERNEST HEMINGWAY

For me, the most memorable episode in this novel is when the fish first appears. The description of the great purple marlin emerging from the sea has an enormous impact and the rest of the story will centre on the relationship between these two 'characters' – the old fisherman and his catch.

This is the biggest fish that the old man has ever come across, and he has doubts about whether he can physically land it in his small boat. Hemingway describes this struggle in considerable detail and we live each moment with the old man.

In short, this is a tale that will hold your attention and move you as well. The style that Hemingway uses is quite different from anything I had ever read before, and it has made me think about the art of storytelling. I believe everyone at college should read this unique work of fiction, for although it was written several decades ago, it remains strangely relevant today.

(171 words)

6 Set the review for homework.

Units 13–18 Revision

SB pages 122–123

Lesson plan
Topic review   10–15 minutes
Vocabulary   15–25 minutes
Grammar   15–20 minutes
Phrasal verbs   20–30 minutes

SV   Omit the Topic review and set the Phrasal verbs quiz for homework.
LV   Ask students to write a short composition, 100 words, on one of the subjects in the Topic review. See also Extension activity for 1.

The aim of this unit is to go over some of the main points covered in Units 13–18. With the exception of the Topic review, this unit can be done as a test or for homework.

Topic review

1   In pairs, students look at questions a–j and talk about whether the statements are true for them or not. Encourage them to go into detail, not just say 'yes' or 'no', and to recycle structures and vocabulary they have covered in the preceding units.

Extension activity

Make a 12 x 12 square crossword grid and ask each student to make a crossword using five down and five across clues. The words asked for should all be in Units 13–18.

They should then give their crossword to another student to do for homework.

Vocabulary

2   This is exam practice for Paper 1 Part 1.

Answers
1 A   2 C   3 B   4 C   5 C   6 B   7 C   8 D

Grammar

3   Students need to read through the sentences and correct them. The mistakes include grammatical errors, punctuation and vocabulary. Some sentences have more than one mistake.

Answers
a   There is too much traffic in our town.
b   I have such a lot of / so much work to do, I don't know where to start.
c   The Netherlands and Austria are both countries in the European Union.
d   Her house, whose roof is thatched, is twelfth century. / Her house, the roof of which is thatched, is twelfth century.
e   John plays the piano and he also plays football, whereas his brother prefers playing chess.
f   Let me give you some advice / a piece of advice – don't go on a journey/trip without checking whether you need a visa or not.
g   There's a man over there who has been watching us for about half an hour.
h   I have lived in Las Vegas for ten years and I still find it exciting.
i   By this time next year, I will have taught / will have been teaching for twenty years.
j   He asked me where the police station was.
k   I saw a flash of lightning when I was out in the garden.
l   Have you got enough information to object to the factory noise?
m   He's the one to whom I gave the book. / He's the one who/that I gave the book to.
n   My eldest son, who lives in Paris, is a physicist.

4   Students need to match the sentence beginnings a–g with the endings 1–7.

Answers
a 5   b 3   c 7   d 4   e 1   f 2   g 6

Phrasal verbs

5

Answers and other possible answers
1   B an operation, a relationship that's ended
2   A someone's career, the market for e-books
3   B an idea, a plan, an answer, an explanation
4   C an adventure
5   A at an airport
6   B e.g. hours, days, months
7   A
8   C sugar, chocolate
9   A a meeting, something you've arranged to do but don't want to
10 A interest rates, the number of students going to university

94   UNITS 13–18 REVISION

19 An apple a day ...

19.1

Exam skills	Speaking Paper 4 Parts 2 and 4
Grammar focus	Modals: advice and suggestion
	It's time
Vocabulary	Topic set – parts of the body
	Phrases with *on*

19.2

Exam skills	Listening Paper 3 Part 4
Grammar extra	*to have/get something done*
Exam skills	Reading and Use of English Paper 1 Part 1
Vocabulary	Word formation
	Topic set – health

Workbook contents

Reading and Use of English Paper 1 Part 5 – multiple choice
Vocabulary – health
Reading and Use of English Paper 1 Part 4 – key word transformations
Writing – essay

19.1 SB pages 124–125

Lesson plan

Speaking	10–15 minutes
Grammar	45–50 minutes
Vocabulary	15–20 minutes
SV	Omit 5 and 6.
LV	See Extension activity for 3.

Speaking

1   *An apple a day ...* is part of the English saying *An apple a day keeps the doctor away.*

This speaking activity is similar to the one in Paper 4 Part 2. Ask the students to compare the photos, giving reasons why they think the people have chosen the particular activities. They should then discuss the other questions.

Modals 3

2   The aim of this questionnaire is to elicit phrases associated with advice and suggestion. Ask students to read it through and choose their answers. Where there is no exact answer for them, ask them to choose the answer that is closest for them. They should add up their score at the end and compare results with another student. The results are not meant to be taken seriously!

3   Ask students to underline the verbs and phrases in the 'How did you score?' section which are used to express advice and suggestion. They should pay particular attention to the structure which follows. For example:
You should + infinitive without *to*
If I were you + *I would* + infinitive without *to*
You ought + *to* infinitive

Refer students to the Grammar folder, page 174.

Answers
Mostly As
You are fairly healthy and have a good attitude to life. <u>You should try</u> to watch what you eat a little more, and <u>if I were you, I'd try</u> to do a little more exercise. Too much work and not enough play isn't good for you! I think <u>it's about time you thought</u> about your diet.

Mostly Bs
You are obviously in the peak of condition! <u>I recommend you relax</u>, as <u>you ought to get</u> some rest, even if you don't need much sleep. Overdoing things can lead to illness! <u>Why don't you try doing</u> more reading, or go on holiday – or <u>have you ever thought of playing</u> a musical instrument?

Mostly Cs
Oh dear! <u>It's time you took</u> a good look at your lifestyle. Missing meals and not getting enough sleep and exercise are very bad for you. <u>My advice to you is to start</u> right away – <u>you'd better join</u> a gym. <u>I also suggest cutting down</u> on coffee and drinking more water and fruit juice. Too much caffeine will keep you awake!

Students should now work with a partner and take it in turns to give advice and make suggestions in response to problems a–h. Anything appropriate will do here.

Possible answers
a   You ought to see if you're allergic to something.
b   You should run it under the cold tap immediately.
c   Why don't you do extra cycling practice?
d   If I were you, I'd go straight to hospital.
e   You'd better check if you need any injections.
f   What about putting your head between your knees?
g   I recommend you put some vinegar on it.
h   My advice to you is to see your doctor.

4. The expressions *It's time*, *It's about time* and *It's high time* are often tested at *Cambridge English: First* level. They express strong advice or opinion. The past tense used after these phrases is, in fact, the subjunctive. It is not referring to the past, but to the present.

Draw students' attention to the Corpus spot.

Suggested answers
(Students might use *he* or *she* in their answer, which is fine.)
a It's (about/high) time you gave up smoking.
b It's (about/high) time you walked a bit more.
c It's (about/high) time you read a book occasionally.
d It's (about/high) time you applied for another one.
e It's (about/high) time you ate something healthier.
f It's (about/high) time you bought your own house.
g It's (about/high) time you had it mended.
h It's (about/high) time you bought your own.
i It's (about/high) time you got up earlier.
j It's (about/high) time you bought a new one.

Vocabulary

5. Ask students to look at the photo of Rafael Nadal (a Spanish tennis player) and name as many parts of the body as they can.

Answers
a jaw   b wrist   c eyebrow   d elbow   e chest
f waist   g thigh   h knee   i ankle

6. This is a matching exercise. It also recycles the second conditional. There may be some debate about what is the right thing to do in each case.

Suggested answers
If I broke my leg, I'd have it put in plaster.
If I had a headache, I'd take an aspirin.
If I cut my knee badly, I'd have stitches.
If I grazed my elbow, I'd get an elastoplast / a plaster.
If I sprained my ankle, I'd put a bandage on it.
If I had flu, I'd go to bed.
If I had a cough, I'd take some cough medicine.

7. Draw students' attention to the phrase *on holiday* in the 'How did you score?' section. Explain that the phrases in the box are frequently tested and should be learnt.

Answers
a on average   b on behalf of   c on purpose
d on duty   e on condition that   f On balance
g on offer

Ask the students to try to use the expressions when they say whether the statements in the exercise are true for them or not.

19.2 SB pages 126–127

Lesson plan	
Listening	20–30 minutes
Grammar extra	10 minutes
Use of English	10–15 minutes
Vocabulary	20–30 minutes

SV   Set 6 and 7 for homework.
LV   See Extension activity for Grammar extra.

Listening

1. Ask the students if they know what the four types of alternative medicine mentioned here are.

Background information
Homeopathy – a method of treating disease with small amounts of remedies that, in large amounts in healthy people, produce symptoms similar to those being treated
Osteopathy – therapy based on the assumption that restoring health is best accomplished by manipulating the skeleton and muscles
Reflexology – a therapeutic method of relieving pain by stimulating specific pressure points on the feet and hands
Herbal medicine – a medicine made from plants and used to prevent or treat disease or promote health

2 Acupuncture is a type of treatment that has been used in Chinese medicine for over 4500 years. It is now an important part of alternative medicine in many parts of the world. Acupuncture involves controlling the body's flow of energy, known as chi, in this way encouraging the body to heal itself.

3 The students should look at the photos and talk about them. They show a man having acupuncture and someone being treated with reflexology.

4 🔊 **2 15** Students are going to hear part of an interview with a doctor. The doctor is being interviewed about acupuncture. Students should look carefully at the questions before they listen to the recording. Remind students that some of the answers may be true, but are not the right answer if they do not answer the question.

> **Answers**
> 1 C   2 B   3 A   4 B   5 A   6 A   7 B

Recording script

Interviewer: Good morning. On the programme this morning we have Dr Sylvia Carpenter, who is a family doctor. Dr Carpenter, you're a great believer in Chinese medicine, aren't you?

Doctor: Yes, I am. When I was a medical student I spent a wonderful month at a hospital in Hong Kong, where they use acupuncture as well as Western medicine, which is, of course, what I was studying. I saw how effective acupuncture could be, especially for people with digestive disorders, asthma, back pain or stress.

Interviewer: Now, you're not qualified to practise acupuncture yourself, are you?

Doctor: Oh, I'm just an ordinary GP or General Practitioner. I work in a small community, with about 3,000 people on my list. In the past we only referred patients to specialists at the local hospital for treatment – you know, to have their chests X-rayed or have a blood test done. Now I often suggest they see an acupuncturist as well, if I feel it would be of benefit. I can't actually recommend one specifically, but I keep a list of qualified ones.

Interviewer: So, say I go to see an acupuncturist about my backache. What would happen to me?

Doctor: Well, first of all the acupuncturist will ask you for very detailed information, not just about your medical history, but about your lifestyle, what you eat, what sort of exercise you do, how much sleep you get. The treatment you need is then decided and he or she will insert needles in various parts of your body. If you have a back pain, you won't necessarily have a needle in your back, though. It might be in one of your limbs – maybe in a knee or a wrist.

Interviewer: How often would I have to go?

Doctor: It depends on your problems. For some conditions, one or two treatments a week for several months may be recommended. For less acute problems, usually fewer visits are required. There aren't usually any side effects. You might feel worse for a couple of days, but that just means the treatment is working. It's quite common to feel exhausted after the first treatment, and this can be overcome with a bit of extra rest.

Interviewer: Now, the big question. Does it hurt?

Doctor: Well, it'd be wrong to say 'No'. It depends where the needles are inserted. Some areas are more sensitive than others. Once the needles are in place, there's no pain at all.

Interviewer: Are any positive benefits all in the mind, do you think?

Doctor: No, not at all. Acupuncture has been successfully used on cats and dogs. These animals don't understand or believe in the process that helps them to get better. A positive attitude towards the treatment may reinforce its effects, just as a negative attitude may hinder the effects.

Interviewer: It's a relatively new type of treatment, isn't it?

Doctor: Only in the West. It was first discovered in China in 2696 BC! In 1671 a French Jesuit priest wrote about his experiences in China and was the first Westerner to see acupuncture in use. In 1820 acupuncture was actually being used in a Paris hospital! Acupuncture received a lot of publicity in the West when James Reston, a reporter for the *New York Times*, was covering the visit of President Nixon to China in 1971. Reston developed appendicitis and his appendix was removed using acupuncture as the anaesthetic. He felt no pain during or after the operation because of acupuncture. But, in some ways, your question was right. Acupuncture is still a fairly new subject in the West, but growing all the time.

Interviewer: Thank you, Dr Carpenter. Now we're …

Grammar extra

This part of the unit deals with causative *have*. Point out that *to get something done* is more informal than *to have something done*.

Answers

You have something done because it is something that you don't normally do yourself and you need someone else to do it for you.

a to have your clothes cleaned
b to have your hair cut/styled
c to have your car serviced/repaired
d to have a dress or other item of clothing made/altered
e to have a suit made/altered
f to have your nails done/polished
g to have your teeth checked / a tooth filled
h to have some furniture repaired/made

Extension activity

Ask students to imagine they are millionaires with lots of servants. They should think of what they would have done for them. For example:
I would have my breakfast brought to me in bed.
I would have my bath filled with champagne every day.

5 Ask students to look at the photo of someone doing yoga. Ask them to tell you what they know about yoga. Do any of them do it themselves? If they are not sure what it is about, some background information can be found in the text itself.

Make sure that students read through the text a couple of times before they try to answer the questions.

Answers
1 A   2 B   3 B   4 D   5 B   6 A   7 B   8 C

Vocabulary

6 This exercise can be set for homework if time is short. The sentences are all taken from the interview. Students need to change the form of the word in capitals so that the sentence makes sense.

Answers
a believer   b specialists, treatment   c medical
d effective   e various   f sensitive   g successfully
h operation

7

Answers
a sweat   b surgery   c ward   d scar
e bruise   f examination   g bug   h symptom

Ask students to form groups and to tell a story using as many of the nouns connected with health as they can. Begin: *Last week I woke up in a hospital ward.*

Exam folder 10

SB pages 128–129

Paper 1 Part 5
Multiple choice – fiction

Explain that in Paper 1 Part 5 there is sometimes an extract from a novel or short story. The advice for fiction and non-fiction is exactly the same. There is no difference in how the students should go about answering the questions.

Answers
1 C   2 B   3 D   4 B   5 A   6 C

20.1

Exam skills   Reading and Use of English Paper 1
               Part 6

20.2

Grammar focus   Gerunds and infinitives 2
Vocabulary   Topic set – crime

Workbook contents

Listening Paper 3 Part 2 – sentence completion
Vocabulary – word formation
Reading and Use of English Paper 1 Part 2 – open cloze
Grammar – gerunds and infinitives
Writing – error correction

20.1 SB pages 130–131

Lesson plan

Speaking   20–30 minutes
Reading   40–50 minutes

SV   Set 5 for homework.
LV   See Extension activities for 2 and 6.

Speaking

1   Ask the students to look back at the end of Unit 7 to remind themselves of some useful language.

    The five photographs show clues in a police case and are (left to right): a fingerprint, a hair being removed from an item of clothing, a tyre track, a glass with fingerprints and some liquid in the bottom, and a DNA analysis.

    Put students in pairs and ask them to decide which two clues are the most reliable, giving reasons for their choice. If they are not sure what DNA is, they just need to say so. It is included here so that students have a chance to see something they are not familiar with and realise they can say they don't know. They will be familiar with the other clues, so they can talk about them.

2   Here students have four questions which they should discuss in groups of three. Help them with vocabulary or other relevant questions. The conversation can go on to talk about capital punishment or the death penalty.

Background information
In the UK, the death penalty used to be carried out by hanging. This was abolished in 1965, although this decision has been reviewed occasionally by parliament.

Extension activity

Put these categories on the board: Car People Property Money

Ask students to say which of the following crimes go in which categories. (There is more than one answer, depending on your point of view.)

kidnapping	hijacking	shoplifting	joyriding
burglary	speeding	con tricks	bank robbery
manslaughter	drug pushing	pickpocketing	vandalism
blackmail	arson	mugging	rape
fraud			

Suggested answers
Car
joyriding – stealing a car and driving it fast for fun
speeding – going too fast
People
kidnapping – taking someone away by force usually for money or political reasons
rape – sex with someone without consent
manslaughter – killing but not with any plan to do so
con tricks – confidence tricks – telling someone a story to trick them out of money or goods
mugging – assaulting someone in the street and stealing from them
drug pushing – selling illegal drugs
Property
shoplifting – stealing from shops
burglary – breaking into a building to steal
arson – burning a building
vandalism – destruction of property
hijacking – taking control of a plane or other vehicle, usually with violence
Money
fraud – cheating a company or people to obtain money
bank robbery – stealing from a bank – usually violently
mugging – see above
pickpocketing – removing money from someone's pocket
blackmail – using information to obtain money from someone
con tricks – see above

To round up this exercise, students, in groups of three or four, should decide which five crimes they think are the worst and put them in order (1 = the worst).

Reading

3   Some of the more difficult vocabulary from the article
    is studied here so that students can understand its
    meaning before doing the reading task.

    Students can use an English–English dictionary to decide
    which word or phrase fits in the gaps in sentences a–g.
    They may have to change the form of the verb.

    Answers
    a a forensic scientist   b the proof   c guilty
    d genetic code   e evidence; the suspect
    f to cover your tracks   g taken to court

4   The article is about detecting crime. It is practice for
    Paper 1 Part 6.

    Answers
    1 G   2 F   3 C   4 A   5 E   6 B

5   Students discuss their views in pairs.

6   This exercise practises back reference. This is tested in
    Paper 1 Part 5.

    Answers
    a the traces of evidence   b the old techniques
    c an item   d the dusting of surfaces

Extension activity

Students need quite a lot of practice in linking pronouns with
what they are referring to, both forward and back references.
It is a good idea to spend some time looking at pronouns in
newspaper and magazine articles for extra practice.

20.2 SB pages 132–133

Lesson plan	
Listening	20–30 minutes
Grammar	40–50 minutes
Vocabulary	10 minutes
SV	Set 4 and 6 for homework.
LV	See Extension activity for 3.

Listening

1   **2 16** In Unit 7, students looked at verbs which were
    followed by an infinitive or gerund. The aim of this unit
    is to introduce verbs which take a gerund or an infinitive
    with a resulting change of meaning. Many of the verbs
    are heard on the recording.

    Before students listen to the recording, they should read
    through questions a–j very carefully.

Answers
a   72 months
b   in a car park
c   so he could take his friends on holiday/vacation
d   when he was working near the bank
e   He wanted a lot of people who were all dressed like him
    to be outside the bank because it would confuse the
    police.
f   He pretended to work as a landscape gardener outside
    the bank.
g   on a tyre/raft down the river
h   because a lot of people were wearing the same clothes as
    the robber
i   Curcio had left some things when he had been rehearsing
    the robbery and they were found by a homeless man and
    given to the police.
j   DNA on a bottle that matched DNA on a mask.

Recording script
Good morning. Here is the news. Anthony Curcio, 28, of
Monroe, Washington, was sentenced today to 72 months
in prison for robbing an armored car in Monroe. Curcio,
a former star athlete in high school, who earned college
scholarships in basketball and football, carefully planned
the robbery over nearly a year. Curcio was arrested in a
car park following a spending spree at a shopping mall.
At the trial, Curcio stated that he had needed the money
from the robbery to pay to take his friends on an 'all
expenses paid' vacation to Las Vegas.

According to records filed in the case, Curcio first
came up with the idea of robbing an armored car while
working for his parents' landscaping company. They
were doing some work near the Monroe branch of the
Bank of America and Curcio studied the deliveries that
the armored car made every week. At the same time,
he decided on the best ways to escape after the robbery.
He manufactured a disguise with clothing that could be
easily removed, and even strung a cable in a nearby river
so that he could use an old tyre as an inflatable raft and
pull himself down the creek away from the scene of the
crime.

Curcio decided to use an open WiFi network to put an
advertisement on the internet offering men a potential
job. The open WiFi was to enable him to post things on
the internet without the police being able to trace him.
Applicants for the job were told that they had to stand
outside the Bank of America in Monroe at a certain time
on a certain date and wear specific clothing. This was
to consist of a blue shirt, yellow vest, safety goggles and

work shoes. They were told that there was construction work available for whoever turned up.

On the day of the robbery, Curcio wore a wig, safety goggles, work boots and a tear-away blue shirt and <u>he pretended to be a landscaper cutting weeds outside the bank</u>. When the armored car arrived, it stopped outside the bank to unload the money and the delivery person got out. Curcio stopped working and then sprayed the delivery person in the face with pepper and stole a bag containing approximately $400,000. Curcio remembered to remove his wig, face mask, work clothes and hat and threw them in bushes before <u>making his escape on the inflatable raft down the river</u>. What initially confused police was <u>the group of people at the scene all dressed in the same clothing as the robber</u>.

However, the FBI and Monroe Police were soon on Curcio's trail. According to police, three weeks before the robbery took place, <u>a homeless man had seen Curcio trying out his ideas for the robbery. Curcio had arrived in a wig and gone through what he would do on the day of the robbery. Before leaving in his car, he had then dropped the wig and an empty bottle behind a trash can at the bank. The homeless man had reported Curcio's license plate number to police and given them the items he had found behind the trash can.</u> The police found out that the car was registered to Curcio's wife. Nothing was done at the time as there was no crime to connect it to, but the police had kept the items.

When news came of the attack on the armored van at the bank, a police sergeant remembered getting the earlier report. Investigators retrieved the drink bottle from storage and found it had a sample of DNA on it. They then compared it to the DNA from the face mask and wig left by Curcio a short distance from the scene of the real robbery. <u>The DNA from the bottle matched the DNA from the items left at the scene.</u> The police then began following Curcio and finally arrested him in the car park.

Some $220,000 of the stolen money was recovered following Curcio's arrest. He pleaded guilty to all charges. In asking for a five-year sentence, Assistant United States Attorney Bruce Miyake said that, and I quote, 'All robberies are inherently violent and serious. This robbery stands out for its boldness, level of planning, and its ingenuity. As has been seen, Curcio was obsessive in his planning. This, however, led to his ultimate downfall.'

2

Gerunds and infinitives 2

3   Refer students to the Corpus spot and example. They should then read the information in the box and look in the Grammar folder, page 174, to check on the difference in meaning.

Extension activity

Students usually need quite a bit of practice in the use of these verbs. When they have looked through the Grammar folder, give each of them one of the verbs which change meaning. Tell them to write down two sentences which exemplify the meanings. They then have to read their sentences out loud and explain the difference in meaning. This can be done in teams, as a class or in pairs.

Students could also try to retell the robbery story from memory, taking it in turns to tell the story or listen for mistakes.

4 When you are happy that students are clear about the use of these verbs, they can do the written exercise.

Answers
a fitting   b reading   c to inform   d walking
e to hurt   f to pay   g telling
h drinking and driving / to drink and drive
i to keep   j to talk   k to do up   l running

5 This exercise revises the work done in Unit 7 and this unit. If time is short, it could be set for homework.

Answers
1 to make off   2 to be   3 to fasten   4 checking
5 to see   6 to avoid   7 carrying   8 to put
9 reporting   10 lead   11 know   12 to sign

6

Answers
a hang – all the others are to do with freeing
b illegal – all the others are adjectives which normally describe a person
c arrest – all the others are forms of crime
d jury – all the others are guilty
e trial – all the others are places
f offence – all the others are what happens after you are caught
g commit – all the others are what the legal system does to you

Writing folder 10

SB pages 134–135

Paper 2 Part 2 Emails

Remind students of the importance of writing in a consistently appropriate register – in this case, informal. Encourage students to use a full range of language.

1   Give students time to read the exam question and then refer them to the Assessment focus. Elicit their ideas on structural range for this piece of writing.

2   Ask students to read the sample answer and find examples of the structures they have ticked.

> **Answer**
> All areas are covered (note that passive forms are not generally appropriate to informal writing, but the example here – *you're faced with a difficult challenge* – is perfectly acceptable).

3   Ask students to work in threes, each finding one type in the answer.

> **Answers**
> *Phrasal verbs*: stick to, cutting out, checking out, giving up, work out, going for
> *Prepositional phrases*: between you and me, in (great) shape, in fact, (keep) in touch
> *Adverbs*: radically, more regularly, incredibly

4   Stress the value of using words with prefixes and suffixes, which demonstrates vocabulary range.

> **Answers**
> **a** temporary   **b** expect   **c** understand   **d** disappearance
> **e** unbelievable   **f** recommendation   **g** passionate
> **h** carelessly

5   Ask students to read the exam question and elicit their content ideas. Set the email for homework.

> **Sample answer**
> Hi Nicky
>
> Sorry to hear you are facing a bit of a problem with unwelcome guests! I know how tiny your apartment is and I guess it must be really difficult sharing such a small space. If it was me, I'd never have invited them to stay in the first place. You're too nice, you know!
>
> Anyway, I'd say you have to get tough with these people – they're really taking advantage of your good nature! Give them a deadline and make it clear they'll have to have found somewhere else to live by that date.
>
> In the meantime, make sure they help out with the cleaning, and insist they cook a meal or two as well. You're out at work all day, so it's rather unfair of them to expect you to play the perfect host when you get home.
>
> Above all, you shouldn't worry about hurting their feelings – after all, they're not close friends, so it doesn't matter if you fall out over this, does it? They sound as though they are behaving totally unreasonably.
>
> Let me know how you get on.
>
> Love,
>
> (184 words)

21 Urban decay, suburban hell

21.1

Vocabulary	Collocations
Exam skills	Speaking Paper 4 Parts 2 and 4
	Listening Paper 3 Part 2

21.2

Grammar focus	Mixed conditionals
Exam skills	Reading and Use of English Paper 1 Part 1
Vocabulary	Topic set – buildings
	Word formation

Workbook contents

Reading and Use of English Paper 1 Part 6 – gapped text
Grammar – mixed conditionals
Reading and Use of English Paper 1 Part 3 – word formation

21.1 SB pages 136–137

Lesson plan

Vocabulary	10 minutes
Speaking	10 minutes
Listening	30–40 minutes
Speaking	20–30 minutes

SV   Omit 6; students choose one discussion statement only in 8.

LV   Allow more time for discussion in 8.

Vocabulary

1   Ask students to put the relevant words into the four sets under the headings Buildings, Leisure facilities, Services and Transport. Write answers on the board. Students will hear some of the nouns in the Listening section.

> **Answers**
> **Buildings**
> property value, construction work
> **Leisure facilities**
> art gallery, shopping mall, community centre / shopping centre
> **Services**
> rubbish collection, road maintenance, street lighting
> **Transport**
> traffic jam, congestion charge, residents parking

Speaking

2   The pictures show a street in Greenwich Village, New York, and a suburb in Melbourne, Australia. Allow students to complete one long turn (and brief comment from the other candidate), but tell them when one minute has passed.

Listening

3   **2 17** Play the first part of the recording and elicit what the woman's profession is.

> **Answer**
> She is an architect.

> **Recording script**
> **Julia:** My name is Julia Banks and I'm here today to defend modern, high-rise architecture. Those who criticise this type of living accommodation claim that it is unnatural – the argument goes something like this: If we were meant to live up in the sky, we would have been born with wings! Well, as an experienced architect, I obviously challenge this view. The fact is that many people have to opt for high-rise accommodation, and our profession has a responsibility to design homes that are fit for them to live in.

4   **2 18** Elicit students' predictions. Then play the Part 2 recording.

> **Possible predictions**
> 1   a person/organisation
> 2   a word that collocates with *regulations* e.g. *official*
> 3   a type of housing, e.g. *flat*
> 4   something connected with new buildings, e.g. *bricks*
> 5   an example of an environmental requirement
> 6   something that means the same as *urban sprawl*
> 7   something that collocates with *facilities*
> 8   something relating to architecture in a city centre
> 9   something that might exist downstairs in a building, e.g. *shop*
> 10   something in cities that may make people unhealthy, e.g. *pollution*

> **Answers**
> | | | |
> |---|---|---|
> | 1 government | 2 planning | 3 tower block |
> | 4 material(s) | 5 heating | 6 suburb(s) |
> | 7 out-of-town | 8 skyscraper(s) | 9 jazz club |
> | 10 (heavy) traffic | | |

Recording script

Julia: There's no doubt that things have improved over time. We look back to the high-rise buildings of the 1960s, where people were sometimes uprooted from established communities and forced to live in ugly concrete blocks against their will. Yet we should remember that this was a time when many people wanted to be rehoused because their living conditions were so bad. And <u>this was a policy upheld by government</u>, rather than decided by architects.

So, the situation has changed for the better. It seems that lack of consultation over new buildings is rarely an issue with the public nowadays. The fact of the matter is that <u>there are much tougher planning regulations in place</u> than was previously the case.

I should underline my personal experience here. For six years of my childhood, <u>I was in a tower block</u> in quite a run-down part of Bristol, so I do know what it's like. That's largely what drove me to become an architect, actually. Yes, some 60s architecture is poor, but the point is, if it hadn't happened, we would be making similar mistakes today, whereas, as it is, we have been able to learn from it and move on.

For one thing, <u>the buildings being put up today generally have better materials</u> than in the past, certainly in comparison with the 1960s. A lot more thought goes into this aspect, with the upside that new buildings look more attractive as a result.

Then there are the environmental considerations. We have to design buildings that are efficient, so <u>for us in Britain that means paying particular attention to things like heating</u>. Of course, that particular requirement wouldn't be an issue for architects in southern Europe.

<u>Something that does trouble me is 'urban sprawl', by which I mean the endless suburbs.</u> And their existence is at a huge cost to the tax-paying public in terms of upkeep – basic services like drainage, road maintenance, that sort of thing. City expansion isn't very good news for the countryside either. At the same time, there's sometimes appalling decay in the middle of our cities as a direct result of this move outwards. <u>Shops in the centre have closed because of out-of-town facilities</u>, and people are forced to drive when once they bought locally. That's not sustainable, is it?

What I believe in – and what many architects are trying to work towards – is the regeneration of our city centres, but <u>this can only happen if we think vertically – design skyscrapers, in other words</u>. There's no space to do anything else! It's a really exciting development that could breathe new life into our cities.

<u>Imagine if your building was a multi-use one, where you just go downstairs to a jazz club</u>, or across the street to pick up some late-night shopping ... this is the upmarket housing of the future, where no one will need to own a car.

In a recent radio phone-in, 67% of callers thought that the car should be banned altogether from central London. I truly think people are ready for this. <u>They understand that traffic is slowly killing us</u>. Living in the city has to become a healthier and more acceptable option.

Background information

There is now a congestion charge for most motorists wishing to drive into the centre of London. Any chargeable vehicle entering the congestion charge zone between 7 am and 6 pm has to make a daily payment and fines are enforced for non-payment. Several cities worldwide have referred to the London scheme when developing their own plans for city centre traffic.

Play the recording again so that students can check their answers. Pause after each question has been covered. The relevant part of the script is underlined for each question.

5 Elicit answers to a–e.

Answers
a T She says: *It seems that lack of consultation over new buildings is rarely an issue with the public nowadays.*
b T She says: *For six years of my childhood, I was in a tower block in quite a run-down part of Bristol, so I do know what it's like. That's largely what drove me to become an architect, actually.*
c T She says: *City expansion isn't very good news for the countryside either.*
d F She says: *What I believe in – and what many architects are trying to work towards – is the regeneration of our city centres*
e T She says: *In a recent radio phone-in, 67% of callers thought that the car should be banned altogether from central London. I truly think people are ready for this.*

6 Students listen again for the words with *up*.

Answers
a 3   b 5   c 1   d 2   e 4

Speaking

7

Answers
a 2 b 1 c 1 d 2 e 3 f 2 g 1 h 3
d is too direct for a discussion and might give offence.

Elicit other examples of the three categories.

Suggested answers
Other non-verbal strategies for directing a conversation include nodding or shaking one's head; making eye contact; raising a hand; leaning forward.

8 Students now discuss the statements as described, using some of the techniques in 7. Remind them to change roles after every statement. Monitor their use of turn-taking and give them feedback on this at the end.

21.2 SB pages 138–139

Lesson plan	
Grammar	40–50 minutes
Vocabulary	30–40 minutes
SV	Keep 5 brief and set 6 for homework.
LV	See Extension activity for 5.

Mixed conditionals

1 Ask students what the term 'mixed conditional' might mean (a conditional structure that does not follow the standard types but uses different tenses). Then ask them to identify the tenses used.

2 Allow students three to four minutes to write out the full sentences. Then ask for examples. Write up some on the board, correcting them if necessary. Be sure to explain why you are making any corrections.

Possible answers
a … would look much worse.
b … wouldn't be starving now.
c … would be less well-informed.
d … wouldn't be stuck in this traffic jam.
e … would still be living at home.

3 Ask students to look at the example. They can finish these sentences in pairs and then report to the class.

Answers
a would have chosen to live in them in the first place.
b would have finished your essay by now.
c wouldn't have been so high for the last 20 years.
d would have gone out at 3 am this morning to buy you some paracetamol.

Refer students to the Grammar folder, page 175.

4 Point out the sentence openers in bold and check students understand them. Ask students to match the sentences in pairs.

Answers
a 5 b 3 c 6 d 1 e 2 f 4 (mixed conditional)

5 Remind students to use turn-taking skills in their discussion.

Ⓔxtension activity

Suggest that students work in groups to prepare a set of posters on city life. Some groups should feature the disadvantages covered in 5, while others could focus on the advantages of living in a city.

Vocabulary

6 The photo shows the central dome of the Reichstag, designed by Norman Foster.

Answers
1 C 2 C 3 B 4 A 5 D 6 A 7 C 8 B

7

Suggested answers
• structure, construction
• enlarge, expand, extend
• enormous, extensive, huge, vast

8

Answers
rebuild; reconsider/reconsideration; regenerate/regeneration; reopen/reopening; repay/repayment; repossess/repossession; rewrite

a regenerated   b reconstructed/rebuilt   c reopening
d reconsider

Exam folder 11

SB pages 140–141

Paper 1 Part 7
Multiple matching

Ask students to read through the Exam advice section. It is useful for students to have a highlighter pen so that they can highlight the part of the text with the answer in.

This text is about four people's attitudes to driving.

Tell students to read the questions and then scan the texts for the answers. When they finish, they should compare answers with another student.

Answers
1 D   2 A   3 B   4 D   5 C   6 B   7 A   8 C
9 B   10 A

22 A world of music

22.1

Exam skills	Speaking Paper 4 Part 2
	Reading and Use of English Paper 1 Part 6
Vocabulary	Topic set – music

22.2

Grammar focus	Concessive clauses
	Complex sentences
Exam skills	Reading and Use of English Paper 1 Part 1

Workbook contents

Reading and Use of English Paper 1 Part 1 – multiple-choice cloze
Vocabulary – music
Writing – gapped clauses
Listening Paper 3 Part 1 – short extracts

22.1 SB pages 142–143

Lesson plan

Speaking	20–30 minutes
Vocabulary	10 minutes
Reading	35–50 minutes

SV	Limit discussion in 3 and 9.
LV	Use Extension activity after 9.

Speaking

Ask how many in the class enjoy listening to music or playing it.

1   Ask students to look at the two pictures. They show an open-air music festival and a special event where 2,740 young musicians played in the Birmingham Symphony Hall.

   Allow students three minutes to compare the pictures.

2   **2 19** Remind students of the format of the Speaking test and of Paper 4 Part 2, referring them to the explanation on page 8 if necessary. Explain that on the recording they will hear two students at *Cambridge English: First* level, Carmen and Jurgen, together with an Interlocutor (the examiner who asks the questions). Carmen will be doing the long turn and Jurgen will comment briefly at the end. Ask students to listen out

for the views of both students. Either play the recording straight through or pause after the long turn to summarise Carmen's views.

Answer
Jurgen prefers taking part, whereas Carmen says she enjoys being part of a large audience and listening to music.

Recording script

Examiner: Carmen, here are your two photographs. They show a lot of people in one place. Please let Jurgen have a look at them. Carmen, I'd like you to compare these photographs, and say how you would feel in each situation. Remember, you have only about a minute for this, so don't worry if I interrupt you. All right?

Carmen: Yes, fine. Well, the pictures have two things in common. The first, which you mentioned, is the huge number of people. The other is that they both show music taking place. This one is at a major rock festival – it's outdoors, of course. The other one is indoors and it looks like an enormous orchestra. There must be hundreds of performers there, I mean er ... there are over a hundred cellists taking part! I don't know where it is but all the musicians are quite young, so maybe it's a concert organised by several schools?
The main difference between the two scenes is that in the first one, there is an audience – people are watching a band on stage – while in this one, everyone is a performer. I really like being part of a large audience, sitting back and relaxing to the music.

Examiner: Thank you, Carmen. Now, Jurgen, which situation would you prefer to be in?

Jurgen: Oh, the orchestra, definitely. I'd rather participate than watch music. I actually belong to a large choir and we sing as a group of about a hundred and twenty. It's really good fun, and because there are so many of us, it doesn't matter if you make a mistake sometimes.

Examiner: Thank you.

Elicit comments on the recording: is this long turn more difficult or easier than they expected? Reassure them if necessary!

3   Ask students to discuss their ideas in pairs, encouraging them to give extended answers.

Vocabulary

4 **2 18 ◁** Play the recording again for the vocabulary check. Many of these words will come up in the gapped text which follows.

Note that the word *gig* is informal and is only used to refer to modern music, e.g. pop, jazz.

Answers
Perform: take part, participate
Performers: musician, orchestra, cellist, choir
Performance: concert, festival

5

Answers
a violinist   **b** pianist, piano player   **c** drummer
d saxophonist   **e** trumpeter   **f** flautist

Reading

6 Elicit brief suggestions from students as to what a *tribute band* is.

Answer
A tribute band is a group of musicians who play the music of a famous pop group and pretend to be that group.

7 Ask students to go through the main text as suggested. Give them a maximum of five minutes for this stage.

8 Ask students to complete the gapped task.

Answers
1 F   **2** B   **3** G   **4** D   **5** E   **6** A

9 Allow students to discuss the questions in pairs and elicit answers from the class.

Extension activity

Use the internet to research further information about tribute bands in English. Students could vote for their favourite tribute band, or suggest a new tribute band that they would form themselves.

22.2 SB pages 144–145

Lesson plan
See note below.
Grammar   60–70 minutes
Use of English   5–20 minutes

SV   Set 6 and 7 for homework.
LV   Review answers in 7.

This lesson focuses on ways students can produce more complex sentences, particularly in their writing. All of the material could be done at home and reviewed in a later class. If you do this, check answers or hand out copies of a key.

Concessive clauses

1 Elicit answers from students.

Answer
The underlined words introduce information that contrasts with that in the main clause.

Answers
1 c   **2** e   **3** b,d   **4** e   **5** a,e   **6** a

2

Suggested answers
a Although the concert was supposed to start at 8.00, it actually started at 9.30. OR The concert was supposed to start at 8.00, although it actually started at 9.30.
b The group did a lot of dancing on the stage, though it was very small. OR Though the stage was very small, the group did a lot of dancing (on it).
c Despite still being a member of Blur, Damon Albarn is in the band Gorillaz. OR Damon Albarn is in the band Gorillaz, despite still being a member of Blur.
d Even though I can't get to many gigs, I manage to keep up to date by watching YouTube. OR I manage to keep up to date by watching YouTube, even though I can't get to many gigs.
e While you are allowed to use the school instruments in the music room, they should not be taken away from there.
f Even if we miss the first band, we'll still get to the festival in time for Arctic Monkeys. OR We'll still get to the festival in time for Arctic Monkeys, even if we miss the first band.

Complex sentences

3

Answers

Putting the reason first makes for a more cohesive and logical piece of writing.

Example **a** starts with a conjunction.

Other conjunctions used in this way are *because* and *since*.

4 Refer students to the Exam spot and encourage them to vary the way they start sentences when speaking and writing (as the candidate has done in 5).

5 Ask students to read the candidate's paragraph and notice how the sentences are constructed.

Answers

Although I like almost everything about music starts with a concessive clause – highlighting a choice.

In the sentence *Seeing blues or soul bands in concert is one of the things that I really enjoy*, the underlined extended noun phrase is put at the beginning to give it particular emphasis.

The adverb used three times is *really*. Other adverbs that could be used instead: *especially*, *particularly*.

6

Suggested answers

a Since it was late, we decided not to stay for the final band.

b Beautifully made by hand and reddish brown in colour, the cello has an excellent sound.

c Having learnt the recorder for three years, Ellen then went on to the flute.

d Despite its technical brilliance, the trumpeter's playing has neither energy nor emotion.

e Due to the conductor's mistake, the soloist had to miss out a whole verse.

7 Suggest that students do this Paper 1 Part 1 task individually and then compare answers. Alternatively, it could be set as homework.

Answers

1 B   **2** D   **3** D   **4** A   **5** D   **6** B   **7** C   **8** D

Writing folder 11

SB pages 146–147

Paper 2 Part 2 Reports

1 Refer students to the introductory information about reports. Then ask them to read the exam task and the report. They should discuss improvements in pairs, working through a–d. Remind them to use complex sentences in **d**.

> **Answers**
> **a** Add something to make it clear what the report is about, for example *on last year's festival.*
> Add a concluding sentence, for example, *I hope you will find this information helpful.*
> **b** The site
> Catering facilities
> **c** The underlined parts of the answer are too informal.
> To the festival organisers
> People were forced to go from one end of the site to the other when buying food and drink, which they were not pleased about.
> This would give the festival useful additional funds.
> It is clear that a bigger site and better organised catering are needed, as well as some changes to the timing of the event.
> **d** Even though there was some car parking, many people had to park ...
> Although there was some choice of catering at the site, very little vegetarian food was offered.
> People seemed to enjoy the performances, so perhaps each band ...
> Since several members ... thought the tickets were unusually cheap, the price could be raised next year.

3 In pairs or small groups, students decide on suitable types of shopping for each of the target groups.

> **Suggested answers**
> **1** f, h, i   **2** a, d, j   **3** c, e, j   **4** b, d, g

4 Check that students understand what is required and explain that before they write the report, exercises 5 and 6 provide useful language input.

5

> **Answers**
> **a** competitive   **b** bargain   **c** fortune   **d** purchase
> **e** economical   **f** savings   **g** budget   **h** expense
> **i** brand   **j** stock
> The adjectives are *competitive* and *economical*.

6

> **Answers**
> **a** brands   **b** competitive   **c** stock   **d** budget
> **e** fortune   **f** bargains

7 Suggest students use key words in the task rubric for their headings and plan paragraphs on food, study materials (books and stationery) and souvenirs, so that their report will look similar to the sample answer in 1. Remind them who the target reader of the report is.

> **Sample answer**
> This report covers the main shopping facilities in Newtown.
> **Food**
> There are two supermarkets: Coopers, selling luxury brands of food, is only five minutes from the college and has a large car park; Shopsmart, on the edge of town, is bigger and usually has the most competitive prices, but is difficult to get to. It is best to buy fresh fruit and vegetables in the market, which is held every day apart from Sunday.
>
> **Study materials**
> In Bridge Street, there are four bookshops, where you'll find a good range of dictionaries in stock. For those on a tight budget, there is a huge stationery shop in the main square, where you can buy everything from files and pens to software. There is a small bookshop on the college campus, which also sells basic stationery items like paper.
>
> **Souvenirs**
> Newtown doesn't have as many souvenir shops as London, but the castle has its own shop, and so does the museum. Additionally, things on the market stalls won't cost a fortune, so your students can hunt for bargains there.
>
> I hope this report will be useful for your students and I wish them a pleasant stay.

23.1

Speaking	Talking about natural phenomena
Exam skills	Listening Paper 3 Part 2
Vocabulary	Phrasal verbs with *off*
	Words often confused
Exam skills	Reading and Use of English Paper 1 Part 2

23.2

Grammar focus	*I wish / If only*
	wish and *hope*
	as if / as though
	would rather
Exam skills	Reading and Use of English Paper 1 Part 4
Vocabulary	Word formation with *un-*
	Topic set – weather

Workbook contents

Vocabulary – weather
Reading and Use of English Paper 1 Part 7 – multiple matching
Grammar – *I wish / If only*

23.1 SB pages 148–149

Lesson plan

Speaking	10 minutes
Listening	20–30 minutes
Vocabulary	30–45 minutes

SV	Set 4 and 6 for homework.
LV	See Extension activity for 4.

Speaking

1 Ask students to discuss the photos in pairs. They then have to decide which set of vocabulary items goes with which photo. Check they understand the vocabulary.

Answers
1 volcano – **c**   2 lightning – **a**   3 floods – **b**
4 earthquake – **d**

2 Ask the students to form different pairs and discuss a–c.

Listening

3 🔊 2 20 A woman is talking about an experience she had when she went camping with her brother some years ago. This is practice for Paper 3 Part 2. Students need to complete the sentences with a word or short phrase.

Background information
The talk is based on a true story of what happened when Mount St Helens in Washington State in the USA erupted in 1980.

Answers
1 forest fire   2 smoke cloud   3 silent   4 handle
5 the tent   6 (some) (tree) branches   7 shirts
8 (hot) ash   9 rotten/bad eggs   10 radio

Recording script

Liz: Thank you for asking me here today to talk about what happened to me and my brother Dave when we went on a camping trip.

On the morning of May 18th, 1980, we were camping about 18 kilometres from Mount St Helens in Washington State in the United States. I was making coffee over a wood fire and Dave was fishing down in the creek. I saw him look up at a small black shape on the horizon. He shouted that there must be a forest fire – it couldn't be a storm, as we knew that rain wasn't forecast. Within 30 seconds the thing was absolutely enormous and then it just kept getting bigger and bigger and coming at us faster and faster, and it became very dark.

All I could think was that I wished I were somewhere else! It wasn't like a smoke cloud, it was as if it were alive and it was massive and dense, and very black. It was the strangest thing you can imagine. It was totally silent until it got down into the canyon where we were and then there was a huge roaring. I remember looking at the fire and the wind just blew the flames low along the ground, and watching the handle of my coffee pot just kind of melt in the flames, and then this awful cold – it just surrounded us. The funny thing was that the spoon inside the pot was just fine.

I wasn't just frightened by then, I was absolutely petrified, and so was Dave. Well, we started to run back towards the tent. Stupidly I thought that if only we could get in the tent, we'd be safe! Then the thing hit us. It was … it was like a bomb going off and I fell over backwards and was covered with dirt. I remember wishing it would stop and almost immediately it did, and then Dave reached over to me and asked me if I was OK. We got up and realised that there were trees all around us. In fact, we'd fallen down into a hole left by the roots of a tree and then some branches had covered us. Dave tried to climb out of the hole but it was too hot. Then, when we did get out we were met with such a scene of total destruction. Everything had happened so fast. When we set off it was difficult to breathe, so we took our shirts off and wrapped them around our heads. There were flashes of lightning across the sky at that point too. Wet towels would have been better, but needs must, as they say.

It was really hard to get out of the valley because the ash was nearly a metre deep and it was so hot underneath you could only stay in it for a short period of time. Then we had to get up on a tree stump and take our shoes off and unroll our pants, but within a few minutes they would be filled up again. There was a terrible smell – like rotten eggs, not smoke or burning wood. Anyway, we were really lucky. We could easily have been killed. I wish now that we'd taken a radio with us, then maybe we would have had some warning. Even a couple of hours' warning would have helped. I had my cell phone with me but there was no signal in that valley. We went back a few days later and found the site where our tent had been. Thank goodness we fell in that hole!

Vocabulary

4 These phrasal verbs all have *off* as the adverbial particle.

> **Answers**
> 1 going off – exploding
> 2 took off – removed
> 3 set off – began the journey
>
> a Tom *told* the boys *off* for throwing stones at the windows.
> b The Prime Minister's visit to Australia has been *called off* because of the floods at home.
> c Anne *sent off* fifty job applications before she got an interview.
> d The excitement of living in New York soon *wore off* and then I felt homesick.
> e The village was *cut off* because of the flooding.
> f My sister *broke off* her engagement to Pete yesterday.
> g The thief was *let off* by the magistrate as it was his first offence.
> h I *logged off* my laptop and went to bed at about midnight.

Extension activity

Students should write out sentences of their own which show they know how to use these phrasal verbs correctly.

5 Students often confuse the meaning of the words in this exercise. Ask the class to use an English–English dictionary and work through the sentences.

> **Answers**
> a in the end   b invaluable   c nowadays   d raised
> e Lie   f Tell   g cook   h stolen   i injured
> j sympathetic   k sensitive
>
> The differences can be explained as follows:
> a we say *at the end of the story/film/book*
>   *in the end* = finally
> b *priceless* = so valuable it has no price
>   *invaluable* means very useful and is usually used about something abstract like help or advice
>   *valuable* = worth a lot of money
> c we use *nowadays* when we talk about something that is happening currently
>   *actually* = in fact
> d *to raise* – transitive – takes an object
>   *to rise* – intransitive – no object
> e *to lie* – takes no object
>   *to lay* – takes an object – *to lay eggs, to lay the table, to lay your head on a pillow*
> f to tell someone something
>   to say something to someone
> g *a cook* is a person
>   *a cooker* is a machine
> h *to steal something from someone*
>   *to rob somewhere or someone of something*
> i *to damage something*
>   *to injure someone*
> j *sympathetic* = kind and understanding if you have a problem
>   *friendly* = pleasant and sociable
> k *sensible* = full of common sense
>   *sensitive* – used about someone who feels very deeply

6 Ask students to read through this article about volcanoes carefully before they start to fill the gaps. This exercise can be set for homework.

> **Answers**
> 1 in   2 without   3 over   4 called/named
> 5 the   6 which/that   7 was   8 this

23.2 SB pages 150–151

Lesson plan	
Grammar	40–60 minutes
Vocabulary	20–30 minutes
SV	Set 7 and 8 for homework.
LV	See Extension activity for 4.

I wish / If only

1   Unit 19 looked at expressions with time which are followed by a verb in the past tense. This unit deals with *wish, if only, would rather* and *as if / as though*.

Refer students to the Grammar folder, page 173 for more details. Students usually readily understand the use of *wish* + past perfect for past regrets. They have problems with *wish* + past simple and *wish* + *would*.

Students need to think of five other things Liz would have wished after the eruption.

Suggested answers
I wish we had realised the mountain might erupt.
I wish there had been a cave nearby.
I wish we had left the area before the eruption.
I wish we had never decided to go camping.
I wish it hadn't happened to us.

They then need to move on to talk about themselves and the things they regret doing or not doing.

2   Students have to talk about what they wish for at this very moment, using *wish* + past simple or *could*.

3   *Would* after *wish* or *if only* is usually used for complaints or criticism. Ask students to write down some examples of things they are annoyed about at the moment. For example:
I wish the teacher would stop giving us so much homework.
I wish my parents would send me more money.

4   *Wish* is often confused with *hope*. *Hope* is usually a wish for the future and usually takes a present tense with future meaning.

Answers
a   I hope the rain stops soon.
b   I hope you can come to my party.
c   I wish I could speak Arabic.
d   I wish Peter would finish writing his book.
e   I wish I had remembered to bring the sleeping bags.

Extension activity

If possible, record the news in English from the BBC World Service and get students to take notes. They should then form pairs and talk about what they wish and hope for their country or the world as a result of what they have just heard.

Corpus spot

Refer students to the Corpus spot and then ask them to correct the sentences.

Answers
a   I wish I had **known** it two days ago.
b   I wish you **had been** there with us.
c   I hope you **can** give me some more information. / I **wish you could** give me some more information.
d   I **hope** you can come to Japan. (it's possible the person will be able to go to Japan) / I **wish you could** come to Japan. (it probably isn't possible for the person to go to Japan)
e   I **hope** (that) you have a good time.
f   I **wish** I could help you out a little bit. (the speaker doesn't think they will be able to help) / I hope I **can** help you out a little bit. (the speaker thinks they will be able to help)
g   I wish I **hadn't** said that.

5   a   The use of the past tense after *as if / as though* is for hypothetical situations – they express unreality.

b   *Would rather* has a similar meaning to *would prefer to*.

6   This exercise is exam practice for Paper 1 Part 4. If time is short, this exercise can be set for homework.

Answers
1   wish (that) I had taken
2   would/'d rather the children stayed
3   only we had seen some
4   wish (that) I lived / could live
5   wish (that) you wouldn't / would not
6   would/'d rather you didn't / did not

Vocabulary

7   The negative prefix *un-* is often tested in the exam and is a useful prefix for students to know at this level because of its frequency of use. Remind students that it combines with different parts of speech – adjectives, adverbs, nouns and verbs (see Exam folder 2).

> **Possible answers**
> a   a knot, shoelaces
> b   a cardigan, a jacket
> c   a knot, shoelaces
> d   a parcel
> e   a secret, a clue
> f   a Roman coin, treasure
> g   a belt, a seat belt, a hair clip
> h   a door, a suitcase, a cupboard
> i   a ball of string

8   Students will probably need help with this exercise. If they are finding it difficult, you could fill in some more of the letters to help them. It could be set for homework.

> **Answers**
> a   tornadoes   b   tropical   c   boiling   d   forecast
> e   freezing   f   poured   g   hurricanes
> h   drought   i   damp, humid

Exam folder 12

SB pages 152–153

Paper 1 Part 5
Multiple choice – non-fiction

Ask students to read through the Advice section for Exam folder 10.

There are various types of item which are tested in this part of the Reading paper:
*   detailed understanding
*   global understanding
*   backwards and forwards reference
*   vocabulary

The questions are all in text order, with the global question, if there is one, at the end.

This article is about a woman who goes on a painting holiday to Africa. Ask students to read through the article to get a general feeling of what it is about. They should underline the words or sentences that they think contain the answer and when they have finished, they should discuss their answers with a partner.

> **Answers**
> 1 D   2 C   3 A   4 B   5 B   6 B
> 1   Although I can make a try at it with words, trying to paint it in my sketch book is another matter altogether.
> 2   I certainly don't want a man capable of such things looking at my own awful brush-strokes.
> 3   To begin with, it seems that he considers me a fellow artist.
> 4   I grew up in places like that, and I connected with it immediately.
> 5   wonderfully organised; reclaim the land; rebuild farmhouse; lay foundations; etc.
> 6   The answer is B. The holiday wasn't totally unsuccessful. Although the woman meets another artist, there is nothing about learning to work with others. The article isn't really about travel.

24 Anything for a laugh

Topic Humour

24.1

Exam skills	Speaking Paper 4 Part 2
	Reading and Use of English Paper 1 Part 7
Reading	Guessing unknown words through context
Grammar extra	*rather*

24.2

| Grammar focus | The grammar of phrasal verbs |
| Exam skills | Reading and Use of English Paper 1 Part 2 |

Workbook contents

Reading and Use of English Paper 1 Part 3 – word formation

Vocabulary – humour

Listening Paper 3 Part 4 – multiple choice

Reading and Use of English Paper 1 Part 4 – key word transformations

24.1 SB pages 154–156

Lesson plan

Speaking	15–30 minutes
Reading	40–50 minutes
Grammar extra	10 minutes

SV Omit feedback stage in 1; omit 4 and set Grammar extra for homework.

LV Give feedback in 1 and extend discussion in 4. See Extension activity after 5.

Speaking

1   Monitor students as they carry out their long turns and, if time permits, feed back on their performance afterwards. The photos show:

  1   Mr Bean (actor Rowan Atkinson)
  2   a scene from the Wallace and Gromit animation film *The Curse of the Were Rabbit*
  3   clowns performing in a circus tent
  4   a street performer on a tiny bicycle cycling through a ring of fire

Reading

2   Ask whether students know any urban myths. Then give them a minute or so to read through the questions and prepare to scan the texts.

3   Give students 20 minutes to complete the task on their own. Elicit answers and deal with any problems by referring to the relevant parts of the texts.

> **Answers**
> 1 B   2 A   3 D   4 C   5 A
> 6 D   7 B   8 D   9 A   10 C
> The relevant words in the texts are given beside each answer.
>   1   B   he found he only had about £5
>   2   A   he'd dropped a metal milk crate on its head
>   3   D   paid no attention
>   4   C   the petrified couple tossed all their money at him
>   5   A   rushed off to hospital to have their stomachs pumped
>   6   D   carried on puffing
>   7   B   go home or get a quarterpounder
>   8   D   ignoring the company's no-smoking policy
>   9   A   disguised the damage with ... lemon and cucumber
>   10   C   a note saying: 'I'm real sorry ...'

4   Students discuss their views in pairs.

5   Reassure students that difficult words in the exam texts will not cause them problems, providing they look at surrounding context to help them guess the meaning. It is unlikely that the underlined vocabulary here (which is all above B2) would be tested on Paper 1.

> **Answers**
> **a** loomed   **b** retained   **c** bewildered   **d** tossed
> **e** shooed ... away   **f** all the trimmings   **g** settled*
> **h** scruffy   **i** fleeing   **j** crates
> *The English Vocabulary Profile Wordlists show that certain senses of the verb *settle* are within B2, for example the intransitive meaning of LIVE, to start living somewhere, and the transitive DECIDE, to decide or arrange something. However, *settle* with the meaning of PAY, as in *to settle a bill* or *a debt*, is less frequent and not known until the C levels of the CEFR.

Extension activity

Write these examples from texts A and D on the board: *gasps of admiration, a wad of cash.* Explain to students that when a noun is followed by *of* and a second noun, the meaning will be linked. Elicit other phrases, giving students the first part, for example:
a pile of (books, leaves, rubbish)
a spoonful of (flour, honey, sugar)
pieces of (broken pottery, chocolate, paper)
thousands of (angry people, happy faces)

Grammar extra

Explain that the texts contain several examples of *rather,* a useful word in English.

Answers
a 1 than   **b** 3 would; not   **c** 2, 4 quite

24.2 SB pages 156–157

Lesson plan
SV   Set cloze text for homework.
LV   Extend 3 by referring to the Phrasal verbs list on pages 164–5, asking students to find more phrasal verbs that match the statements.

The grammar of phrasal verbs

Note: the approach taken to phrasal verbs through this course has been to focus on meaning and use. In this final unit, students are shown the underlying grammar of phrasal verbs.

1   Check understanding of the term *intransitive* before students spend a few minutes thinking about the examples. Elicit answers from the class.

Answers
d and **g** contain intransitive phrasal verbs.

2

Answers
b no change possible
e Also possible: He put down the snack ...
f no change possible
h no change possible
i no change possible
j no change possible

3

Answers
1 d, g
2 f, j
3 b
4 c, e – h is an exception (we do not say 'put a fight up')
5 a, i

4

Possible answers
a turn off the TV   **b** get it over with   **c** made out a car
d has put me off   **e** picked up Swedish   **f** look them up
g worked out the answer   **h** faced up to the problem

Corpus spot

Encourage students to record phrasal verbs in this way, adding common noun phrases as they come across them. Elicit other noun phrases for each phrasal verb – for example, *catch up on + the ironing, my work, some reading,* etc.

catch up on some sleep
come up with some good ideas
keep up with the international news
live up to his expectations
put up with your bad moods

5   Ask students if they know any jokes that they could explain in English. Write up any vocabulary which arises. Then suggest they do the matching task in pairs.

Answers
a 10   **b** 7   **c** 15   **d** 9   **e** 4   **f** 13   **g** 2   **h** 8
i 11   **j** 5   **k** 1   **l** 12   **m** 6   **n** 14   **o** 3

Ask students which jokes they think are the best, and which are the worst. Take a class vote.

6

Answers
1 during/in   **2** at   **3** though   **4** up
5 be   **6** most   **7** for   **8** since

Writing folder 12

SB pages 158–159

Paper 2 Part 2 Articles

1   Ask students to read the exam question. Ask which live entertainers they admire and elicit the reasons why they are impressed by them. Then refer students to the factfile on Eddie Izzard, who is quite well-known across the world for his stand-up comedy act and other roles.

2   Ask students to underline the mistakes.

3   Refer students to the Corpus spot – the *Cambridge Learner Corpus* shows that these are very typical errors at this level.

Answers
The errors are highlighted, with corrections in brackets.

Eddie Izzard – a man of many talents
Eddie Izzard has been a stand-up comedian for over 30 years and regularly sells out the biggest venues, included (including) the Hollywood Bowl. I've seen one of his live show (shows) and they are hilarious. He loves experimenting with language and delivers also (also delivers) whole performances in French. The touring show *Force Majeure* has taken him to 25 countries around the world.

Not only that, but he has acted in much (many) films and plays, and often appears in (on) TV. The most impressive thing about him is the way he raises money for the (no article) charity. For example, for Sports Relief, he spent seven weeks running marathons, covering more then (than) 1100 miles across the UK with only one day off each week! Even though he had very few (little) training beforehand, he somehow managed to keep going, in spite of be (being) in pain at times.

That's why I respect him so much. Nothing is too challenging for him, from facing a huge live audience to the physical strain of marathon running. He received an Outstanding Lifetime Achievement Award from Harvard University, there (where) he was described as an outstanding member of global society.

4   Ask students to read the exam question and elicit their ideas on content.

5   Suggest that students use some of the words and phrases in a–d in their articles.

6   Set the article for homework.

Sample answer
FLIGHT OF THE CONCHORDS
Flight of the Conchords is a comedy act consisting of two immensely talented guys from New Zealand – Bret McKenzie and Jemaine Clement. As well as being great comedians, they are excellent musicians and write extremely funny songs. I first heard them on the radio, but they have since made an American TV series and appeared live worldwide. Their best performances are on YouTube.

The one that never ceases to make me laugh features the song *Issues (Think about it)*, which sounds a serious topic but is in actual fact hilarious! Part of the reason why their act is so successful is their ability to keep a straight face, even when they are saying the most ridiculous things. For example, in the chat they do before performing this particular song, Bret expresses concern for the future of his children and his wife, who are then revealed by Jemaine as imaginary people!

Both performers have a background in music and are able to copy different styles, making fun of them in a gentle way. Their lyrics also display a special sense of humour. Bret and Jemaine are without doubt the funniest musical comedy duo ever – check them out soon!

(200 words)

SB pages 160–161

Lesson plan	
Topic review	15–35 minutes
Vocabulary	35–35 minutes
Grammar	20–20 minutes
SV	Omit the Topic review, exercise 3 could be done as homework.
LV	Extend the Topic review (see 1).

Topic review

1 Follow the standard procedure, using the Extension activity on page 66 for the longer version.

Vocabulary

2 Suggest that students work through exercises 2 and 3 in three teams of up to five students (have more teams if your class is larger than 15). The winning team must not only finish first but also have the most correct answers.

Answers
1 C   2 A   3 C   4 B   5 C   6 B   7 A   8 B

3

Answers
illness or injury: 1 sprain   2 cough
volcanoes: 3 eruption   4 ash   5 lava
musical instruments:
6 oboe   7 piano   8 guitar   9 flute

crime and punishment:
10 robbery   11 court   12 burglar   13 trial   14 fine
parts of the body:
15 eyebrow   16 waist   17 jaw   18 knee
a flute   b waist   c eruption   d sprain   e fine

4 This article is a true story about a man who was involved in making the Spielberg film *Saving Private Ryan*. Students should read through the text and then decide which form of which phrasal verb should go in each gap. Students will probably find this quite challenging and so this task could be given for homework, to be done with a dictionary.

Answers
1 calling up   2 taken on   3 taken aback   4 bring in
5 work out   6 ended up   7 put off   8 miss out on

Grammar

5 Ask students to work through the task in pairs. If there is any time at the end, have a class discussion on everyday things that might one day become valuable.

Answers
1 not   2 few   3 enough   4 up
5 than   6 at   7 being   8 if

Speaking folder

SB pages 162–163

Paper 4 Speaking

Run through the Advice section with students and elicit the format of the test. If necessary, refer students to page 8.

Unless you have plenty of free time and a spare room to use, this complete Speaking test will have to be done as paired practice in class. Ask students to read the instructions, which would form the basis of what the interlocutor would say. They should swap roles across the two long turns in Part 2.

The Part 2 photographs show:

First turn: Uma Thurman at the Cannes Film Festival premiere of *Pirates of the Caribbean: On Stranger Tides* and Sir Paul McCartney being mobbed by fans after attending a ceremony at the Liverpool Institute of Performing Arts, which he founded

Second turn: a street in a remote village in Nepal and busy traffic in a European city centre

Acknowledgements

The authors and publishers would like to thank the teachers and consultants who commented on the material:

Brazil: Eliane Sanchez Querino (KNOW-HOW); Czech Rep.: Ales Novak; Hungary: Ildiko Berke; Italy: Robert Islam (British School of English), Fiona Line (Modern English); Mexico: Lizeth Jerezano Rodriguez; Poland: Dr Andrzej Diniejko (University of Warsaw); Russia: Tatyana Elistratova; Caroline Cooke, Nick Shaw (Cambridge English Studio), Leanne White; Switzerland: Allan Dalcher;UK: Kathryn Alevizos, David Jay, Julie Moore.

Development of this publication has made use of the *Cambridge English Corpus* (CEC). The CEC is a computer database of contemporary spoken and written English, which currently stands at over one billion words. It includes British English, American English and other varieties of English. It also includes the Cambridge Learner Corpus, developed in collaboration with the Cambridge English Language Assessment. Cambridge University Press has built up the CEC to provide evidence about language use that helps to produce better language teaching materials.

This product is informed by the *English Vocabulary Profile*, built as part of *English Profile*, a collaborative programme designed to enhance the learning, teaching and assessment of English worldwide. Its main funding partners are Cambridge University Press and Cambridge English Language Assessment and its aim is to create a 'profile' for English linked to the Common European Framework of Reference for Languages (CEF). *English Profile* outcomes, such as the *English Vocabulary Profile*, will provide detailed information about the language that learners can be expected to demonstrate at each CEF level, offering a clear benchmark for learners' proficiency. For more information, please visit www.englishprofile.org

The *Cambridge Advanced Learner's Dictionary* is the world's most widely used dictionary for learners of English. Including all the words and phrases that learners are likely to come across, it also has easy-to-understand definitions and example sentences to show how the word is used in context. The *Cambridge Advanced Learner's Dictionary* is available online at dictionary.cambridge.org. © Cambridge University Press, fourth edition, 2013, reproduced with permission.

What's on the CD-ROM

- 12 Progress tests
- Wordlists
- B1 phrasal verb list

System Requirements

- Windows® XP, Windows® Vista, Windows® 7 or Windows® 8
- Mac® OS X 10.5, 10.6, 10.7 or 10.8
- 1024 x 768 minimum screen resolution
- Speakers or headphones
- PDF Reader

Objective First Fourth Edition Teacher's Resources CD-ROM software can be run directly from the disk and does not require installation.

Start the CD-ROM:

Insert the disk into your CD-ROM drive.

Windows PC

- If **Autorun** is enabled on your computer, the software will open automatically.
- If **Autorun** is not enabled, open *My Computer*, right-click on the CD-ROM drive, and then choose *Explore*. Double click on the file Objective-First-Teachers.exe.

Mac® OS X

- Double-click on the CD-ROM drive icon on your desktop to open it.
- Double-click on the *Objective First* icon.

Technical support

For support and updates, go to
www.cambridge.org/elt/multimedia/help